THRESHOLDS

Dorothea Straus

THRESHOLDS

THE BODLEY HEAD
LONDON SYDNEY
TORONTO

Some of the material in this book previously appeared in *Harper's Bazaar*, *Partisan Review*, *House Beautiful*, and *The Philadelphia Enquirer*.

IBSN 0 370 01382 4
Printed in Great Britain for
The Bodley Head Ltd.
9 Bow Street, London WC2
by Lowe & Brydone (Printers) Ltd., London
First published in Great Britain 1972

For Roger

THRESHOLDS

CHAPTER I

WHEN I WAS A CHILD THE THRESHOLD OF MY grandfather's home was the take-off place for a journey back in time. Since childhood has not yet stored its own collection of memories, I entered through that threshold into an atavistic world experienced only in my imagination but as real to me then and now as are the recollections of my own life.

I visited my grandfather on Sunday morning and since all Sundays are related, when now I walk down Park Avenue on a cold clear New York City winter's day, the sunlight sharp as a knife, the wind gusting among the tall buildings and the inobtrusive chimes of church bells diminished by the noise of traffic are the same that accompanied me many years ago. Even the knots of people standing sociably on the pavement at the close of the Sunday morning service seem to have been saved from the past in the preservative of a moment's acute recall. It is true that New York has changed; on lower Park Avenue towering glass cubes have replaced the homely apartment houses and at the end of the canyon the vista is blocked by the Pan American Office Building that has absorbed the old Grand Central Terminal in its immense reach. But as I am blown down the street, the familiar turret emerges flattened like a paper pattern against the window-perforated backdrop of the new structure. I approach and the station comes into clear focus like the conjuring up of a castle in a fairy story. Even the clock's moon face has reappeared, pointing distinctly to noon. And the past is resurrected, borne on the wind and shafts of sunlight, caught up by the sound of church bells and automobiles and reinforced by my tingling cheeks and by a pang of hunger that makes me remember the endless roast beef dinners of my childhood that used to be waiting for me at home.

A man is coming toward me, the angle of his black Homburg hat, his polished cane, something about his small compact winter-muffled frame and determined step arrests time's forward beat — it is my father (dead many years), and we are on our way as usual to a Sunday morning visit to my grandfather. His apartment was situated near the station; more broad than tall, the building was spread beneath the terminal like a village under the protection of a castle bastion. The inner court enclosed a square of grass, useless and blank, but I remember it as perpetually green, and combined with the comparative quiet inside, it added to the illusion of a country hamlet within the hurly-burly of the city.

My grandfather's living room was dark, but I knew it so well that although it vanished from my sight when I was ten years old, I can still reconstruct it and place each object in its remembered place. My grandfather would be sitting in his armchair facing the entrance waiting for us. Three immaculate lace antimacassars vied in the obscurity with the dazzling whiteness of his full beard and shining hair. His face was broad and rosy and beamed like a sun at my arrival. On the right of his armchair was a heavy claw-footed mahogany table neatly stacked with newspapers and magazines printed in German script. A carved ivory-handled magnifying glass was always near his hand, and I used to imagine that with its help my grandfather could straighten out the ornate hieroglyphics of the German print into the simple letters I was accustomed to. For many years the magnifying glass survived the passage of time and was relocated, only slightly chipped, on the desk in my parents' library. Since my father's death, it too has disappeared. Although I can still recall the feeling of its carved handle in my grasp and see the thick glass inside its silver ring, it never performed its magic for me and the German script of my grandfather's periodicals remained foreign and undecipherable.

To the left of his chair a door led to the study and bedroom. When our visit was over, Sophie, my grandfather's companion-housekeeper, would appear from that direction. She was a well-preserved middle-aged German lady with a pompadour of gray hair and an enameled face. Sometimes she would show me the array of jars, bottles, and implements that maintained her in her permanently shellacked condition. She had narrow yellow eyes that reminded me uneasily of the sly strength of a fox. The other support of my grandfather's everyday life was his chauffeur, Epting. His form was as crude as Sophie's was subtle. He looked like a pugilist with a hulking frame, close-cropped hair, and a flattened nose. And he could effortlessly hoist my grandfather, himself a stocky man, out of his chair as though he weighed no more than the Santa Claus dolls I played with at Christmastime and transport him for his daily drive in Central Park. I sensed that these guardians made my grandfather shrink into the humiliating dependence of old age and I resented them.

But with me, on the contrary, he seemed to expand, and sitting on a footstool at his knees, I would enjoy my role of youngest and favorite grandchild. For some unknown reason, he would call me in German, "my little goldfish," although a photograph of us taken together on the occasion of his ninetieth birthday party shows me as dark and owlish in contrast to his snowy venerability. He would let me play with his heavy old-fashioned watch and chain ornamented with an onyx fob. It is mine now, lying inert and mute at the bottom of my jewel box. But then it ticked noisily and my grandfather would open the back cover to show me the complicated mechanism inside — so many tiny wheels and pistons working incessantly like a complete factory in microcosm. By far the most fascinating object in my grandfather's living room was a huge oil painting in an ornate gold frame. It depicted a beer hall in greasy browns and blacks. Several fat men were seated companionably around a table with mugs of beer. It was the work of some obscure German painter who had died before its completion, leaving the opened newspaper one of the men was reading a blank that shone out as whitely in the tenebrous beer hall as did my grandfather's beard and the antimacassars in his living room. On Sunday mornings through this painting and my grandfather's reminiscences, I was led back to the little town of Ludwigsburg in the former Kingdom of Württemberg, where my great-grandfather had owned a brewery.

Although I have never been there, a fixed picture remains in my mind to this day. It is always the same, complete in every particular. It appears to me in a pyramidal form, built on a hill with the King's castle and the church at the top, then the garrison with the brewery beneath it, and the fields and farmlands spread out at the base. It is a feudal picture, unashamedly hierarchical, cheerful and intimate in the gingerbread fashion of old German towns. My great-grandfather and his family of six children had living quarters inside the brewery, a solid building of country stone with a pointed gable roof and small leaded windows. Inside the rooms are dark and the constant smell of malt is sometimes mingled with the rich brown smell of venison or hare cooking in the kitchen.

Adjoining the brewery is a beer garden, the town meeting place, especially popular with the soldiers. It is enclosed by a latticed fence and surrounded by fragrant linden trees that shower their leaves down upon the red-checked tablecloths. I see the officers resplendent in gilt-trimmed uniforms gossiping and singing and toasting one another out of thick stone mugs like an opening chorus in *opéra bouffe*.

At this time the King's position was growing unsteady and it became known that the military were planning to unseat him. As they always gathered in the beer garden, my great-grandfather was implicated in the intrigue. Personally guilty or not, he soon found that his brewery was being boycotted and his garden waited sadly empty. This was an intolerable situation and he prepared to act. Deprived of his livelihood as a prosperous brewer, he was even ready to plead with the King. His eldest daughter, Bertha, as aggressively homely as she was garrulous, was chosen for the mission. I picture her wearing her sober but substantial plum silk dress and the scrolled heirloom locket only brought out on state occasions, her black hair drawn tightly like the painted hair of a wooden doll. I see her climbing with determined steps up the steep stony road, past the garrison, past the church — the bells chiming insouciantly — to the baroque portals of the palace. What happened behind those doors is hazy, but the result is known. The interview with the King was a failure, Bertha's quick tongue was of no avail. It is possible that my great-grandfather's judgment was faulty; had Bertha been rosy and dimpled, perhaps her plea would not have been in vain and the history of the family would have been different. At any rate, Bertha's descent was more rapid than her ascent. I used to imagine the momentum of her flight like that of the proverbial witch on the broomstick, causing a great wind that swept the whole family across the sea . . .

I do not remember my father taking part in these reminiscences. He remained in the background, sometimes not even bothering to remove his heavy overcoat and muffler, waiting until we could again resume our interrupted walk in the zestful winter air. Looking back I doubt that his relationship with his father was a close one, yet family duty was strong and Sunday morning always found us here. But I was transfixed by my grandfather's extreme old age and by the knowledge that he had been part of that legendary past. It was as honorific as though an Old Testament patriarch, materialized into rosy flesh and prickly beard, had chosen me as favorite kin. My grandfather would have scorned this fancy. He repudiated all religion with the unquestioning certainty of a bigot combined with a spirit of family conformity. "We were brought up as atheists," he would say with the same pride he displayed when he made me prod the muscles of his upper arms, still hard and bulging "from being apprenticed to a cooper in Brooklyn when I was eighteen years old." In my grandfather's simple categories Atheism was synonymous with Liberalism. And at times family history would be altered slightly and the reason for my great-grandfather's exodus was said to have been his liberal views and insistence on higher wages for his workers. "When the day for departure arrived," my grandfather would relate, "his employees, singing and cheering, lifted my father on their shoulders and carried him through the streets of Ludwigsburg." I do not think my grandfather would have been pleased to know that I confused this scene with a picture of an emperor being transported in a sedan chair high over the heads of his humble people. In this version of family history, Liberalism and Atheism were two virtues that accompanied my great-grandfather, his wife, sons, and daughters on their voyage to America and, like twin talismen, I believed them to be buried under the cornerstone of the brewery transplanted to Brooklyn in 1848.

Like all institutions, the Kupperman Brewery has finally

dissolved, sold to strangers. I no longer know what material remnants survive, and I do not wish to inform myself because I realize they would have little relation to the bright spots of memory I am hoarding. These too will disappear with me, and I hasten to write them down; jagged, inaccurate, distorted as they are, they are still the only monument to be raised against the palimpsest of time.

In my infrequent visits to the brewery during my childhood, the big yellow trucks proclaiming *Rheingold* in oversized German lettering were lined up like an army. When I spotted one in New York City, I would feel a surge of pride and identification like the daughter of a general watching soldiers obey commands. The trucks still move about the streets, still proclaiming *Rheingold* in bold letters, still yellow and shining, but they belong to a foreign regiment and I observe them with the dull detachment reserved for familiar objects grown distant and meaningless.

The business, originally called Kupperman Sons, was renamed *Rheingold* by my grandfather's cousin, David. I remember him as a gnarled old bachelor living the year round in seclusion in a big ugly summer hotel in the suburbs. He had elaborate courtly manners and surprisingly beautiful long-fingered hands that contrasted with his homely face and humped back. I had heard tales of his profligate youth, his addiction to flamboyant low women whom he treated like princesses, wasting the Kuppermans' good money on their keep. David was the black sheep of the family, yet for me he had a rococo fascination. And oddly enough, it was he who had renamed the brewery. Idle, wasteful, set apart from his industrious relatives, it was he, nevertheless, who had stamped those large letters, *Rheingold,* on the family enterprise. And they have endured to this day, while the honest efforts of the other Kuppermans have been forgotten. Family legend tells that David, after attending a performance of *Das Rheingold* (probably in the company of one of those rouged overdressed women, who appeared like weeds to the rest of the family but were for him delicate flowers to be protected), had returned to Brooklyn with the idea of renaming the beer "Rheingold." Inspired by Wagner's Rhinemaidens' song and the flash of gold at the bottom of the river in the first act of the opera, it was David who persuaded the family to drop the name of Kupperman Sons and rechristen the business "Rheingold Breweries." It is odd that they agreed to this. Perhaps, having maintained their financial security and made continuous in Brooklyn the rich golden brew that had its source in Ludwigsburg, the Kupperman family was ready for a sprinkling of culture to adorn their solid bourgeois achievement.

When I was a child the newer aspects of the brewery — its cellars with shining copper vats, bottling plant, office building — held little interest for me. I preferred the stable, dark and vacant, looking like a disreputable jail. Yet once it had proudly housed fifty massive brewery horses. It was here, I knew, that my father, his brother and sister and cousins came after school to watch the unharnessing. Next door there used to be the fascinating blacksmith's shop, the wheelwright, the cooper — a whole industrious cozy world as lusty and alive as the paintings of Breughel. The original office building with its old-fashioned stoop and modest wooden door still stood, but it had been converted into a family lunchroom where I could smell the rich German cooking like the aromas in the beer garden in Ludwigsburg I had created in my imagination from my grandfather's reminiscences. The Kuppermans' homes had disappeared with the family's dispersal and immigration to New York City. But the cobblestones that had paved the area in front of them survived. The rest of the yard used to be floored in dirt and every night a great wooden gate was shut to divide the brewery yard from the residential section. The gate too had vanished, as had the alley of linden trees planted nostalgically by my grandmother. I can picture her (though she died before I was born), an alert bright-eyed woman, pausing behind the correct lace curtains of her parlor window to watch her children outside. Each season is a separate picture: on an autumn morning she could see her husband, sons, and daughter cross the street to office and school. My great-grandfather, though transplanted, had remained obdurately German and had instituted a school in the brewery building for the benefit of his grandchildren and neighboring German-American upper-middle-class families. The master, complete with black suit and starched collar, the rod and ponderous tome, was imported from the old country. It was his habit to guzzle beer from a pitcher while he instructed his class.

In the afternoon the Kupperman children (fourteen cousins) would run back to their homes. The old houses were then in full swing and the linden trees flourishing. My grandmother, always a perfectionist, had grown a wealth of wisteria on the walls of her house. It fell in a thick cascade, and in the spring it blossomed in purple clusters like grapes. Two urns of stiff geraniums guarded her door. Except for these trimmings, the houses were identical, shutter for shutter, stoop for stoop. At the top running across all of them there was inscribed in ornate gold and black script: H. Kupperman Sons — like the baroque decorations on the façades of the houses in a Bavarian town.

In the winter snow blanketed the brewery yard and the cousins played in a sleigh drawn by two white goats. At Christmastime in each house the tree was decorated behind closed doors, thrown open to the children on Christmas Eve. In the morning they found their stockings crammed with nuts, raisins, marzipan, lebkuchen, licorice candy, and special cakes baked for the Christmas season.

When the weather grew warm, the children brought out their velocipedes and peddled up and down the back garden piazza. There were no partitions between the rear porches and they were free to ride the whole length of the houses, occasionally peering into one or another kitchen window to see what was being prepared for supper. Once a week a farmer drove in from outlying Long Island, five miles away. He sat precariously perched on top of his hay wagon with a wicker basket filled with fresh country eggs beside him to be distributed among the families. The hay was thrown up into the stable loft on a long mephistophelian pitchfork.

In July the Kuppermans prepared to leave for the Adirondacks. Steamer trunks were carried down from the attics, furniture shrouded in sheets, and shutters sealed. The urban brewery yard was exchanged for the mountain setting, often wistfully compared by the older members of the family to the unforgettable deep green forests of Bavaria.

When I was a child, my grandfather was the bridge to this far-off world. Although transplanted from Germany to Brooklyn to lower Park Avenue, his venerable squarely built white-haired blue-eyed person suggested the rosy St. Nicholas of German legend — belligerently secular, it is true. Now, years later, I assume that he was for his children at that time merely a problem, a burden that they shared with dutiful conscientiousness. Every third summer, it was our turn to have Grandpa with us. My parents would rent an Adirondack camp and one of the houses was his, presided over by Sophie and Epting. All the buildings were pseudo-rustic log cabins with cavernous rough-stone fireplaces. They were connected by boardwalks and situated between a dark pine forest and a big lake that had a boathouse and a dock at the water's edge. I loved the smell of pine, the sounds of gently dipping oars, and the occasional roar of a motorboat on the lake. The living room walls and furniture were made of birch bark and the gray paint on the verandah steps formed small blisters that could be deliciously exploded by my fingernail. In the forest, evil-looking fungi grew in profusion, smelling of wet leaves, rot, and some fascinating poisonous substance left over from a dark distant elfin world. But we could domesticate them and bring them into everyday focus by etching our initials on their creamy unblemished surfaces. Their smell and the smell of the pine-filled souvenir cushions decorated with Adirondack scenes linger in my memory like remains from a childhood planet someone bearing my name had visited long ago. For my mother, these summers must have been an ordeal as we invariably had a full complement of guests of all ages and, like a hoary cantankerous potentate, Grandfather was always there to be reckoned with. Although he beamed at me, he could, I knew, be stormy and irascible with the adult members of the family. This enhanced his value for me and gave me a sense of importance. "Go see Grandpa. He's in a bad mood today." Feeling like a lion tamer, I would pretend reluctance while secretly pleased with my power.

At mealtime, we would all gather in the dining house at a long table under the glassy stare of a huge moosehead hanging above the fireplace. Grandfather sat at one end in an armchair, my mother at the other. Between them ranged the guests: Miss Schruntz was a piano teacher, tall and rickety, with huge feet and an almost bald pate which showed pinkly through her scanty white hair, reminding me with disgust of an albino mouse. With the cruelty of children I hated her unreasonably and my cousin Agnes and I surreptitiously tormented her at every opportunity, as with the humility of the oppressed she unavailingly tried to please us. There was Agnes' mother, who was divorced and ran a theater school; she was lively and ugly and often proclaimed with histrionic pride, "Everyone tells me I look like Savonarola." Always present were my brother's tutor, a different one each summer — I remember one in particular, Bobby Landon, almost seven feet tall, a college basketball player with a flat nose, white blond hair, and curly long eyelashes that looked like spiders; a French governess for Agnes and me; and transient guests my father brought with him from the city for weekends.

Miss Schruntz, a more or less permanent boarder, tried to earn this hospitality by playing official court jester for Grandfather. Sitting next to him at table, she would address him in German at the start of each meal, "Herr Kupperman, I must tell you a story —" He rarely responded and seemed not to have heard her, while the other adults at the table reacted with exaggerated laughter to cover Grandfather's silence. I, of course, sided with him against Miss Schruntz, and during our rest period Agnes and I would plot new ways to torture her.

But we too attempted to entertain Grandfather. The apex of one summer was a theatrical evening to be given at his house. For weeks we were coached in the boathouse by Cousin Carmen, Agnes' mother. I can no longer recall the play or its author, but I remember that I had the role of a bride to Bobby Landon's groom. The night of the performance Cousin Carmen rouged my lips and painted my eyes with charcoal. I was dressed in white with a long net veil sewn together from a pair of old curtains by the current Mademoiselle. Bobby Landon, a white flower in his buttonhole, wore an unfamiliar city suit, and his unruly blond hair was darkened and sleeked down with water. Only his curly eyelashes, sunburned face, and peeling nose remained of his former self. As we trooped across the boardwalk connecting the boathouse with Grandfather's house, I was able to note, in spite of my excitement, that the mid-August stars were unnaturally large and shining, low enough to touch, like dazzling footlights on an infinite stage. At Grandfather's house I stood behind a screen and waited for my cue. Through the pounding of my heart, I could hear the whispering and giggling of our adult audience and Cousin Carmen's hushing and then Miss Schruntz struck up the first chords of *Lohengrin*'s "Wedding March" and I walked slowly on stage on the arm of my brother, playing the bride's father, toward Bobby Landon waiting at the altar improvised from our sleeping porch night table. I felt above myself and confident of success. If Grandfather was so approving when I was in my ordinary state, now — Suddenly a hoarse cry, "Stop this nonsense at once," interrupted the wedding march and Grandfather's rubber-tipped cane was hurled at the stage and fell clattering at my feet. The players dispersed among the wreckage of the production. I saw Grandfather being half carried from the room between Sophie and Epting. What had happened?

The next morning I overheard Cousin Carmen, always buoyant in a crisis, saying to Miss Schruntz, "Old Mr. Kupperman is too much of a snob to be able to witness even the mock marriage of his favorite granddaughter to a lowly creature like Bobby Landon." Everyone seemed to accept this explanation, but for me it was no answer to my blasted hopes and loss of prestige. For the remainder of the summer, no one mentioned the "theatricals." Everything continued as usual and Grandfather's entertainment was limited to the interminable mealtime stories of Miss Schruntz.

But my moment of elevation and sudden descent left its mark on me, and although I continued to play the role of favorite grandchild, my position no longer seemed so secure.

Many years later, unexpectedly, the answer to the riddle came to me. My husband and I were strolling in our orchard one evening, luxuriating in a new mellow season with its wealth of change and reliable reoccurrence. We admired, one by one, the old apple trees, knobly and bent over under their burden of fruit, and the younger ones planted by us, that had grown from unpromising twigs to slender miniature trees proudly bearing disproportionately large apples or peaches. "There is no use planting anymore," my husband was saying, "we won't be here to see them reach full size." I felt a moment's sadness which changed to helpless anger. And all at once I remembered Grandfather, dead so many years, saw again his cane hurtling toward me. No, it was not snobbishness that had caused his outburst, but the sudden realization of his mortality brought on by seeing me dressed as a bride, masquerading as a woman he would never know, in tawdry imitation of my future he would never see — just as I too was now experiencing an instant's parting of the protective veil that covered the void toward which we are all headed.

The summer I was ten when traveling in Europe, my family received word of Grandfather's death. We had visited numerous German towns with clock towers from which puppet figures in colored robes appeared with hammers to strike the hour. The houses painted outside with bright pictures and German script, the trellised beer gardens, and tables covered in red- and white-checked cloths, the stone beer-filled mugs overflowing with snowy foam reminded me of Grandfather's tales about Ludwigsburg. But we were in a French seaside resort when word reached us. Here the idle hours were filled with walks to and from the beach where the sand was putty-colored and pebbly and the sea usually gray and tranquil. Little French children scampered about in trim bathing trunks, eating their foreign "goûté" of rough bread and milk chocolate, while my brother and I looked on, outlanders, accompanied by the always-present Mademoiselle and tutor, who seemed more obtrusive here on alien soil than they did during our summers at home. The hotel at which we were staying was an imitation palace with a rose garden in the rear laid out in squares and circles like the pieces of a puzzle. The rooms upstairs were furnished in Louis XV, but the satin upholsteries were frayed and faintly spotted, reminders that we were not at home and that other wanderers had lived here before us. It was to this hotel "salon" that we were summoned one morning to learn of Grandfather's demise. Everything was done to spare my brother and me the shocking truths about illness and death. Grandpa, aged ninety-one, had simply gone to sleep one night and did not awaken. I have since heard that it was not as painless as that — also, the casual way my parents told us the news now seems indecent to me. Motivated by kindness and overprotectiveness, they robbed death of its ceremoniousness and Grandpa of the dignity of his longevity. After delivering the news briefly, as though reading from a penny postcard, they told us to go and play on the beach. No one returned for the funeral. Perhaps there was no funeral. And perhaps Grandfather would have approved of this commonsensical, antiseptic attitude toward his death. It is possible it was in accord with his militantly atheistic views. Was my father carrying on a Kupperman tradition in disposing so lightly of his father's death? Did filial respect consist of this apparent lack of respect? I have since wondered about this. But at the time I only knew that Grandfather, my link with that distant past, had disappeared with as little emphasis as the extinguishing of the sun behind a passing black cloud over the gray pebbly beach where we seemed to have been playing without interruption.

. .

I came back from my reverie to the brilliant sun and sharp wind on Park Avenue. The dapper man in the Homburg hat and I crossed paths. Up close his face was hollow as a skull. I shivered. What black magic had transformed him into my father? What optical delusion had endowed this well-dressed skeleton with my father's reassuring appearance? At times the dead return unexpectedly in inappropriate forms to remind us that past and present are divided by tenuous barriers. Yet memory can recapture the years only in glimpses, as tantalizing as the Rhine-maidens' song, as bright as the pile of gold glinting intermittently at the bottom of the river.

CHAPTER II

THE FIRST THRESHOLD I CAN REMEMBER IS ALSO in a New York City apartment — where I was born. I cannot be older than two or three because this earliest memory is associated with the plushy sensation of a beaver cover dropped over my head and shoulders like a muumuu as I sit in my baby carriage, my cheeks tingling from the false country air of a winter's afternoon in Central Park. When the elevator disgorged me and an unremembered nurse at the handlebars of the carriage, I am met by an already familiar room, windowless, lit by electricity day and night. It was called the "foyer" and contained two important almost magical objects, a player piano in which paper rolls unraveled and, according to a language of perforations, made music as the keys jumped up and down without benefit of human hands. What I learned later was Schubert's *Marche Militaire* was my favorite, causing me extreme excitement and delight. I do not believe that my appreciation of music has intensified since that distant point in time. The other object was a reproduction of a Velázquez infanta, perhaps a blown-up detail of the stiff jeweled figure in the foreground of "Maids of Honor."

Out of the foyer another door opened into the "music room," so called because it contained a piano — not self-operating and to me, much less musical than the one in the foyer — and a victrola that had to be cranked like an old Ford car. But this room also had its totem object: on the right-hand wall hung an oil painting of a little girl with golden sausage curls, wearing a blue party dress and high-buttoned shoes and holding a wooden doll similarly dressed in red with sleek black-painted hair. At a later time, this picture had for me the gloomy fascination of an infant's coffin because I had overheard that it was the portrait of my mother's sister, Bessy, who had died at the age of four, before the birth of my mother.

Like an archeologist, I have pieced together my mother's youth from stray objects and scraps of family anecdotes. On my parents' bookshelves I discovered an ancient volume of *Alice in Wonderland* inscribed in a spidery copperplate handwriting, "To Emily On Her Eighth Birthday, from her loving Pappa." When I pored over the quaint, slightly sinister Tenniel illustrations, I felt myself close to the eight-year-old Emily who had become my mother. The opaque barrier of death has always prevented me from imagining any afterlife, and I have substituted the past, prior to my birth, as a backward bid to immortality.

I picture Emily receiving the book from Pappa's hand. Although this grandfather died before I was born I see them both: she with long straight wheat-blond hair, wide-browed with an expression of serious innocence; he, awkwardly tall, prematurely stooped. His birthday greeting to his favorite daughter was loving but formal. The mood of the house was decorous, not gay, and I always visualize the family as beautiful but tinged with melancholy. How many times have I walked past number 12, East Sixty-second Street, altered but still standing. Its flat façade shows no vestigial trace of the high stoop that once led up to the door. I picture the front hall, narrow and dark, with a coatrack that looked like a barren tree, a rubber plant as wooden as the coatrack, and a dim gilt-framed mirror. It was scrupulously clean everywhere but there was the musty smell of old houses — an amalgam of dampness, brass polish, and the aroma emanating from the kitchen underground. The back parlor, also obsolete, was on the first floor. It was a high-ceilinged room, its windows draped in red damask. At either end the bronze heads of Beethoven and Shakespeare on marble pedestals stood guard.

On March 12, 1888, my mother's eighth birthday, the whole family was gathered around the tea table (for the sake of convenience so that I can introduce them all at once). It was the date of the Great Blizzard in New York City, so there were no visitors to celebrate with Emily, except an old aunt who had fought her way through the drifts carrying a box of ladyfingers for the birthday child. The relentless snow outside the drawn burgundy curtains had blanched the city but in my mind's eye the family group appears in vivid colors yet static like Madame Tussaud's waxworks. Mamma presided at the head of the table behind the silver tea urn. She was a beautiful woman in rustling taffeta, her hair dressed in a high pompadour. Her features had the unanimated symmetry of an official portrait. Next came Fanny, the oldest daughter, blond and Junoesque, but always ailing with a malady the family doctor was unable to diagnose. Her bedroom was filled with the medicinal smell of an apothecary shop. She and her husband Edward, nicknamed "le beau" because of his handsome appearance with twirled military mustaches, made their home at 12 East Sixty-second Street because of his inability to earn a living. He worked in his father-in-law's silk business and was tolerated as a member of the family but considered a hopeless failure. Rose was next, she was different from the others, vivid and dark with a reckless smoldering look. Mamma regarded her as "a cross to bear." Richard, the only son, resembled my mother, with the same intelligent wide-set eyes and smooth wheat-colored hair. Sarah, or Sally, was too tall and thin for the current fashions; she was considered the homely one, although today she would be beautiful too. Emily, on her birthday, was seated at Pappa's right, and he treated her like a grownup, with a blend of courtesy and ironic humor. He had an aristocratic Semitic face, with a large aquiline nose and the wide brow he had bequeathed to Richard and Emily. He was a prosperous merchant but he looked professorial and his interests were intellectual and philanthropic. It was he and Emily who loved to browse in the dark library, and he was proud of the bust of himself in the vestibule of the big Jewish hospital on Fifth Avenue inscribed "Our Founder Isaac Frank."

The history of the Frank family is ordinary, consisting of the usual births, deaths, marriages. It is long past, but unbelievably, I have roots in it and it lives on for me, effaced here and there but restorable with the aid of fiction. Shortly after Emily's eighth birthday an event took place which my mother always remembered as a bright spot in her childhood. Its memory has been handed down to me for my lifetime, after which it will be lost in that rubbish heap that time prepares for all such keepsakes: There was whispering in the upstairs hall; outside the tall wooden door of Fanny's room the medicinal smells were stronger than ever. Maids climbed the steep stairs with pots of boiling water and fresh towels, the doctor's coat hung on a peg on the clothes tree in the vestibule. Fanny's husband paced up and down with his hands behind his back, seeming not to know what to do or feel. None of this was so out of the ordinary, but something extraordinary was taking place — Emily knew this — Fanny was giving birth, and at eight, Emily was to be elevated to aunthood. Styles in medicine change like all fashions; today childbirth occurs in an antiseptic hospital world, then the place of birth was the house on Sixty-second Street and all its inhabitants joined in the waiting like spectators at a parade.

"Dr. Walston says it will take a long time. Fanny is having a difficult labor," Mamma announced, anxious but competent, bolstered by the experience of her seven confinements, five living children, two dead.

"Do you suppose it will be a boy or a girl?"

"What time is it?"

"You asked that five minutes ago."

Now and then a moan could be heard, followed by the

reassuring commanding voice of Dr. Walston and footsteps crossing and recrossing the floor of Fanny's room. The routine of the house struggled to carry on but time had assumed the unfamiliar face it wears for big events. The heedless ticking of the grandfather's clock and its chimes announcing the hours were irrelevant — uncomprehending of that endless day.

After midnight Dr. Walston descended, still smelling of chloroform. After the siege he had put on his swallow-tailed coat again, and with his beard and tired, kindly craggy face, he reminded Emily of the lithograph of Abraham Lincoln in her schoolroom.

"Fanny is the mother of a little girl," he said, as though speaking from a podium.

The whole family was permitted to go into Fanny's room. She lay exhausted but victorious against the pillows, with Edward nearby as straight and proud as a Prussian officer. One by one they approached the beribboned bassinet. Emily felt her heart beating as she waited her turn, imagining a pink and white cherub resting on soft covers as on a fluffy cloud. But her heart sank as she tiptoed up to the shrine. There lay a hideous object, shriveled and yellow with a mop of black hair like an old Chinaman. "She is slightly jaundiced," Mamma explained, "and that hair will all drop out." Emily choked back her disappointment and like the others, in tacit conspiracy, murmured words of praise and endearment. But perhaps they were not altogether false. It is possible that the future, like the past, can color the present moment, and maybe behind that ugly baby my mother was able to glimpse, like a double image, the beautiful person who would evolve and the glowing lifelong friendship that aunt and niece, only a few years apart, were destined to enjoy.

Only some of the inhabitants of 12 East Sixty-second Street were known to me. In addition to my mother, there was Uncle Edward and his only child, Irene, Aunt Sarah, and Aunt Rose. Naturally all of them had aged and although they bore the same names, they had little resemblance to the Frank family living in my imagination. Uncle Edward was important in my childhood chiefly for having presented me with a gold bracelet with azure enamel links. I can still feel his waxed mustache scratching my finger as he bent over to kiss my hand, like a European nobleman. Irene was fair, willowy, elegant, perfumed, with a lilting voice. Could she ever have been that ugly saffron-colored infant? The few times I saw Aunt Rose she wore a veil over her ravaged, twitching face. The taut black mesh looked like a wire fence protecting the ruins of a crumbling monument. I had overheard that Aunt Rose "took dope" and she was rarely mentioned in my presence.

My grandmother, known only from hearsay, portraits, and my mother's silence, compounded, I guessed, from lack of sympathy and filial duty, was an inflexibly conventional woman. She ran her large household efficiently and her mirror never failed to return her image as impeccable and handsome in her middle years and old age as in her youth. Her children fitted into the order she created, giving her obedience and withholding the warmth she did not realize was lacking. I see her in the mornings sitting in the parlor, always on the same high-backed chair, stout and regal, receiving the butcher and the grocer for the daily orders. "Good morning, Park and Tilford," she would say, and the grocer would bow grovelingly in deference to her formidable presence and the equally formidable list she was about to present.

It was a small Jewish-American world. Temple was attended on high holidays and the women of the Frank family were noted for being among the most beautiful of the congregation. Religion had become attenuated but occasional attendance was obligatory in keeping with Hannah Frank's position in her limited society. It was part of the ritual of living: the summer trips abroad, spring cleaning, the three o'clock drive in the carriage through Central Park, and the "outfits" to be bought each fall and Easter. In my childhood I was fascinated by a large portrait in an oval frame hanging in my aunt's house. It showed two little girls against a background of whirling snow — my mother and Aunt Sarah. They were dressed in identical velvet coats and hats, one forest green, one burgundy red, trimmed in some dark luxurious fur, and they held muffs up to their pretty rosy faces. They had serious eyes, straight bangs, and long hair, Sarah's auburn (a color that does not seem to exist any longer), my mother's silvery blond.

Hannah Frank did not venture outside the closed circle of her Jewish world and did not expect her children to either. But within that world there were fixed positions below which one did not fall. Everyone was of German descent and a Russian Jew was anathema. The banking and industrial families of greater prominence and wealth than the Franks were looked up to, but they mingled and because of the beauty of the Frank sisters, Hannah Frank could aspire to alliances with them. Also she was complacently aware that though her family was less illustrious than some, it had been in the United States at least a generation longer than most of the leading Jewish families, and in the book of rules that counted. Her daughters would make "good marriages" and her role as mother would be successfully carried out. Only Rose was a worry. She had the reputation for being "fast," her dark beauty was flamboyant, her nature, defiant. She was passionate and unintelligent, with wild hazel eyes that were reminiscent of a pure-bred filly preparing to bolt.

Young gentlemen were received ceremoniously in the Frank parlor. Irene, growing up with her young aunts and uncle, would be sent downstairs to entertain them, while Rose, Sally, or Emily was "getting ready." Everyone knew the value of the little girl with her long golden curls and prim manners in imitation of the older members of the household.

"Will you have a cup of tea while you are waiting? Rose" (Sally or Emily) "will be right down."

"Would you care to see the album of our trip to Europe?"

And she would settle herself on a tufted footstool, her pretty legs in white stockings and high-buttoned shoes precisely crossed.

An anecdote about Irene has been handed down — accurate or not, it has remained intact. It concerns a particular suitor, a member of one of the "elite" families, famous for its great wealth and also for the homeliness of some of its members. The young man was standing in the parlor, smoothing his unruly hair and bristling mustache, when Irene entered with her habitual grace, saying, "Good evening, my aunt will be down soon. Do tell me, are you the ugly Mr. Josephsohn?" We have no record of whether he was the ugly one or not but he must have been the one with a sense of humor because the saying was relayed by him to the rest of the family and eventually, it reached me, too. As a child I enjoyed the image of the impeccable Cousin Irene, a miniature of her poised, polished self, in the cavernous drawing room of the house on Sixty-second Street and I could hear her lilting voice as polite but more treble than the one I knew, saying in all innocence, but for posterity, ". . . are you the ugly Mr. Josephsohn?"

Hannah Frank was indignant; Isaac Frank was troubled and buried himself in his library to avoid his wife's complaints. The whole family felt the reverberations and was aware of the cause. Rose was "going with" an actor! The front door was bolted but she escaped from a first-floor window at night into her lover's waiting arms. There was no stopping her. Like a general, Hannah Frank went to work on a strategy. No one knew how she succeeded, but the house was loud with Rose's sobs and her parents' angry words, "You will compromise the whole family!" "That this should happen after your upbringing!" "No decent man will want to marry you, with your reputation."

Then from somewhere, two new suitors appeared —

brothers — outside the circle of the "good families." James and Sidney Hidell were sleek and a little vulgar, with snapping black eyes, and wore pink carnations in their buttonholes and pearl-gray spats. Ordinarily they would have been frowned upon by Hannah Frank. They were definitely not "*comme il faut*"; perhaps they even were Polish or Russian — but it was imperative that Rose should marry at once and Sally was, unfortunately, quite gawky. Soon the double engagement was announced. Rose married the older brother, James, whom I never met as he was only the first of several husbands. But Uncle Sidney persisted to my day, still sleek, still wearing spats, but the pink carnation in his buttonhole had been replaced by the red ribbon of the French Legion of Honor. Aunt Sarah, towering over him, always looked discontented and contemptuous.

While Mamma ran the practical matters in the house on Sixty-second Street, Pappa, at least for my mother, was its spirit. From her I learned of his intelligence and dry humor, his love of reading and his taste for seclusion, along with his conscientiousness in the performance of civic and charitable duties. He could not have had much in common with his wife or his three older daughters. But with his only son and my mother there existed a close tie based on congeniality of interests as well as strong clan feeling. Pappa, Richard, and Emily formed a separate triangle within the larger circle of family life.

Emily, the youngest, felt a love tinged with admiration for her brother and with awe for her father. It was true that Pappa was often preoccupied, tired, and, sometimes, distant, but when they read together the nonsensical-sense of *The Walrus and the Carpenter,* the mutual feeling of warmth and closeness was all the more rewarding. His familiar, distinguished, tall, stooping figure was a source of pride and comfort to her.

Richard was pure delight. Five years older than Emily, they nevertheless shared many interests: love of music, poetry, languages, and a silent rebellion against the stifling worldly standards of their mother. Richard was the only member of the family who managed to bring merriment into the house. His friends, male and female, imported music and laughter into the dusky library and Emily was often included in their gatherings. She would wait eagerly for the sound of his key in the latch of the front door. And when he went out, the light seemed to go with him.

In the winter of 1896 Richard was twenty-one and Emily sixteen. He was slim, incredibly handsome with his shining helmet of fair hair, newly acquired mustache, and wide-set eyes, so like my mother's. That winter he had moved in a world of balls and operas, but there was also time for study and his beloved violin. The days and nights did not contain enough hours for Richard. Afterward, Emily saw that winter as a spool of precious thread unwinding with uncontrollable speed. Its termination left its mark on her forever.

One snowy evening in February, Richard, on his way to the opera, stopped in the door of the parlor to say good night to his family. He was in full evening regalia, scarlet-lined opera cloak, shining pumps made for the dancing he loved and not for snowy streets. He had had a cough for weeks but he refused to see Dr. Walston, and now Mamma protested that his feet would be soaked. But he laughed at her anxiety and was off to the glories of the Metropolitan Opera House — red velvet, crystal chandeliers, the black and white of the gentlemen's full dress interrupted by the lavish silk-draped nudity of the ladies — all to be obliterated when the lights dimmed, the mysterious overture began, and the golden curtain rose on the birth of time eroticism of the first act of Wagner's *Die Walküre*. Emily pictured all this with longing.

Early in the morning she heard Richard's return. Through her closed door, his hard, dry cough sounded a minor note of dread. Then Dr. Walston's carriage was drawn up to the curb where it remained all day. Richard had caught pneumonia. The next day, the very heartbeat of the house seemed to have stopped — he was worse — and the next, unbelievably, he was dead.

Isaac Frank, broken, dressed in black for the rest of his life, ordered all the blinds lowered in mourning for his son. They were never raised again in the house on Sixty-second Street; all gaiety had fled forever.

I picture my mother during those years living in the darkened house near the father she loved who had become so remote and silent. And I am able to understand that premature lesson in the threat of illness and the finality of death. I can trace her fears in a continuous line that extended into our own family life. I remember her white frightened face at the sound of a cough and her unsteady hand as she held the thermometer up to the light as though Fate were indicated in the slender bar of mercury. The past may be buried but it continues to influence the present. A slight blow on a sensitive area can suddenly uncover it, still recognizable, like the ruins of an interred city.

Those somber years left my mother with a hungry enjoyment of people. When I was a child, she and my father would come to say good night on their way to a party. Then she would always look especially lovely. Sometimes she wore a formal black evening dress, low cut, with a spray of scarlet flowers at her shoulder and an unaccustomed touch of lipstick to match. My father was often grumpy, preferring to stay at home with his family, perhaps to doze comfortably after supper. But my mother seemed gay and eager to go out with my father at her side. Maybe she hoped that with the warmth and chatter of the dinner party around her, she could lay aside for a little while the melancholy sense of danger that was never far away.

After her brother's death, my mother turned more and more to the bright solace of Irene who had been too young to be affected in the same way as the rest of the family. The other source of cheerfulness in the house on Sixty-second Street was Tini, the French maid who had arrived to work for the Franks when Emily was seventeen, a year to the day after Richard's death.

I do not have to invent Tini as I do so much of my mother's early environment, as she extended into my life, only leaving to return to France at the time of my marriage in 1938.

When I was a child Tini's room was a haven. When I

came home from school I ran there first. I would stand at the threshold absorbing the clutter and confusion I knew so well. Tini's past and my mother's were perpetuated here and I was able to sort the strands or roll them together in a colorful blend. The room was small and faced a blank courtyard wall. Near the window was a bureau with snapshots of Tini's family in France: a picture of a first communion that looked bridal, a wretched bride that looked like a first communion — Tini's niece, Alice, another of a small gable-roofed house at the edge of a wood — the house where Tini was born. A framed yellowing photograph of her parents had a sprig of dried wildflowers and a four-leaf clover under the glass. The bureau was covered by an embroidered hand towel and an ivory brush, comb, and mirror set was neatly laid out. Near these, a box that looked like a miniature coffin enclosed Tini's rosary, handsome in jet with a mother-of-pearl cross.

Tini sat by the window in a rocker, sewing, with her feet on a discarded crate. She always saved everything: "Who knows what might not come in useful?" She held her wicker sewing basket in her lap. It contained many treasures. There was a pincushion shaped like a tomato, studded with pins of varying size and shape, a darning egg of smooth celluloid, and a tape measure that snapped into its case like a recoiling asp. When you put your face inside Tini's sewing basket, the cretonne lining smelled of lavender, spice, and age. I used to watch the darning egg slide down the long throat of my mother's stocking. "Tini, tell me a story," I said.

"*Allez, allez,* can't you see I'm busy now?" she would answer with good-natured brusqueness. "If you keep on interrupting me how will I ever earn my pension and retire to Champagney and my rose garden?"

I had heard this too often to be deterred by it. "Tell me about your family-in-France," I said as so many times before.

Tini's family-in-France belonged with the figures in a Gallic fairy tale. Her father had been a forester; to me that meant someone who chopped wood in a jerkin and boots in a thick forest, evil with spotted toadstools. One of her brothers had been a priest; I always pictured him on a bicycle riding through the narrow streets of her hometown, wearing a padre hat and, uncomfortably, a cassock that hid his legs and feet. He had a long loaf of bread for the poor tucked under his arm.

"You have heard about my family so often. They are just plain people," Tini said.

"Tell me just once more how you came to Grandmother's house off the boat from France."

"That was a long time ago. I was pretty then, your *Maman* always said so. I wore a white shirtwaist high at the throat and well boned and a hat with blue flowers that matched my eyes . . . *eh bien tout change, tout casse, tout, sauf le souvenir* . . ."

As Tini told her stories about that faraway time, I was able to illustrate them with the pictures from an old photograph album entitled *Europe — Summer 1897*. On the first page was a picture of two young women leaning against a ship's rail. Its shadow made diagonal stripes across their long skirts. In one corner of the photograph, the nose of a lifeboat and a coil of rope were visible; in another, a triangle of placid sea. Beneath the picture, in a neat schoolgirl's hand, my mother's, was written: "Emily and Tini — S.S. Lahn — 1897." "Colonade and Promenade Karlsbad" showed a raised railinged walk. Portly gentlemen and parasoled ladies were strolling under the chestnut trees in front of the stately portals of the *Kurhaus*. Dignified boredom was the order of the day. Was everyone concentrating on the vagaries of his own digestive tract? "The Posthof Garden" was laid out in formal rows and festoons like a confectioner's wedding cake.

This was the second summer after Richard's death and Pappa and Mamma conscientiously "took the cure," but they never forgot Richard nor put aside their sorrow. Rose, Sally, Emily, and Tini lived through the prescribed three weeks as best they could, whiling away the cloudy tepid days by snapping pictures and gossiping about people now long forgotten . . .

Tini's arrival at 12 East Sixty-second Street fell on the first anniversary of Richard's death and brightened the period of mourning. She brought health and hope where there was grieving and regret.

The house looked the same from the outside: brown stone, high stoop, tasseled curtains looped at the front windows like heavy eyelids. But inside the blinds were down and it was as though the lights were perpetually dimmed. Pappa spent a lot of time in the library, slumped at his desk, his head in his hands or staring at the last smiling photograph of

Richard. He had grown more stooped than ever as though he were ashamed of his own tall body living on now that his son was dead.

It was raining the day Tini arrived and Emily and her sisters were gathered in front of the fireplace in Fanny's sitting room at the top of the house.

"I wonder what she will be like," said Rose. "Anything would be a help to brighten this house."

"Mamma told me she was French — just off the boat and eighteen years old. Her name is Thérèse Garraud," Sally answered.

"Just a year older than I am," said Emily.

"I hope she is gay. We could do with a little gaiety here," said Rose, trying a red bow in the puffs of her dark hair. She studied the effect in the standing mirror, then with an impatient gesture she pulled the ribbon out. "What's the use," she sighed to her reflection. Then turning to Emily, "Let me put your hair up for you. You're too old to have that horse's tail down your back."

"I think Emily looks very nice as she is," said Fanny languidly, stretched out on her chaise longue with the ever-present medicine bottle on a table within reach.

But Rose was already at work brushing out Emily's waist-length hair.

"Now she looks like Alice in Wonderland," Sally said with an edge of sharpness in her voice. She was always aware that she was the least beautiful of the Frank girls.

Emily felt sad. She would be glad when this day of painful memories was over. Tomorrow's ordinariness would be a relief.

They all heard the front door closing and Mamma's dignified heavy step on the stairs followed by an unfamiliar tread, the new maid's. When they reached the landing, Emily opened the door. "We're all in here, Mamma," she called.

Mrs. Frank stepped inside. She was dressed in her afternoon drive costume of stiff black moire trimmed in braid and topped by a white jabot like a blob of whipped cream. The jabot and the gray plume nodding from her hat were the first signs of her emergence from deep mourning. They had just appeared, and to Emily they seemed like the hesitant buds on the bushes in the park, a promise of winter's end.

"Girls," Mrs. Frank said in her correct unemotional voice, "I have brought Thérèse with me." Then turning to the young woman, quiet but alert, who was standing in the doorway, she went on, "Here are Miss Fanny, Miss Rose, Miss Sarah, and Miss Emily."

Thérèse put her straw satchel on the floor, she curtsied briefly, and the cornflowers on her hat bobbed. Emily noticed that her black-fringed blue eyes matched them.

"Bonjours, mesdemoiselles," Thérèse said.

"Thérèse speaks no English," Mrs. Frank explained, "so all of you will have to practice your French."

Rose was still standing brush in hand while Emily was hastily trying to pin back her hair. Thérèse stepped forward, taking the brush from Rose. *"Permettez-moi, Made-*

moiselle," she said. She removed the jacket of her navy blue suit, unpinned her hat, and placed them with extreme care on a marble table top. "*Quelle belle chevelure!*" she exclaimed as she began to brush Emily's hair with deft strokes.

"Will you show Thérèse her room when she is through," Mrs. Frank said. "I am going to have my rest before dinner."

Emily studied Thérèse in the mirror as she worked, while her sisters made polite conversation in their awkward French.

Thérèse had the bright pink cheeks of a country girl and abundant wood-brown hair drawn up from small ears pierced by tiny gold buttons like two shining pinheads. Her nose was pointed and her upper lip showed a faint shadow of down. In her neat white shirtwaist and long dark skirt her figure looked solid, like a little Arabian pony, thought Emily. She is pretty, I like her looks, she added to herself. By contrast, her own reflection seemed colorless — wide-set gray eyes, broad brow, pale mouth.

Emily did not know that she was beautiful, but Thérèse did and she dressed the fine hair with the self-respecting admiration of someone who recognizes quality when she sees it.

"I hope you will like it here, Thérèse," Emily said.

"It's beautiful your America — so many fine things!" Thérèse answered. "I think I will remain a long time."

Emily smiled at Thérèse in the mirror and Thérèse

smiled back. The girls were all talking at once now, telling Thérèse the points of interest she should visit on her "day off."

The fire had warmed the room and with the portières drawn for the evening and the lamps lit, everything looked very solid and cozy. The day had not been altogether bad, after all, thought Emily.

The worn photograph album was crowded with pictures. Cities followed in rapid succession: Berlin, Geneva, Milan, Venice, Paris, London — here a balcony overlooking rooftops, a park gate, a hansom cab, a gingerbread house, a tree-bordered lake, piazza, church spire. Against these varied backdrops the faces of Pappa, Mamma, the girls, and Tini appear and reappear: Emily wearing a straw boater, long-skirted, wasp-waisted, kneeling to feed the pigeons in St. Mark's Place; the birds swarming around her seem to know her gentleness and generosity; Pappa seated by a potted palm, his handlebar mustache and aquiline nose half hidden by some foreign newspaper. On the last page there was a photograph of Tini, silhouetted in a hotel window; in firm profile, she seemed to be looking into the future. What she saw did not dismay or depress her. She will take each day as it comes, equal to what it may bring, confident in her practical optimistic way that "*tout s'arrangera.*"

I reveled in those old-fashioned snapshots and in Tini's sentimental reminiscences. I never tired of hearing about her "chances." She had been engaged to an Irish coachman named Patrick — "as strong as a lion, yet he died of flu in the epidemic." Then, when she was traveling with my grandparents, the proprietor of the best hotel in Berlin had proposed to her. "He was very rich," she always said with a slight note of regret in her voice. He had followed her all over Europe, but she had remained firm. "What, marry a Boche!" she had said. "And live in that *sale pays!* Never! Better to be the old maid I am."

But she never seemed like an old maid to me. She was too individual to be classified and I knew her too well.

After Tini left my family to live with her married niece in her hometown, Champagney, her letters arrived regularly on ceremonial occasions: birthdays, Christmas, New Year's, anniversaries. Her small, firm, pointed writing that looked like fine lace was a link with the past. Sometimes, after my mother's death, she would confuse generations, so that I became Emily and my mother, Madame Frank. She was always nostalgic for my family and I suspected that now that she had at last retired and left the United States forever, we seemed more her own than her niece and her husband with whom she made her home. Her letters made clearings in forgetfulness: I saw Tini wrapping her blue kimono printed with tiny Japanese lanterns around her heavy legs marbled with old veins, as she prepared to climb up into an upper berth, "I wish you would let me sleep up there." *"Va t'en!* This is the way I always traveled. I'm not giving up yet"; Tini cleaning the gravy on her plate with a crust of bread with the same vigor I had seen her use in attacking dust in corners with a broom; Tini offering me Jordan almonds, tasting like sugar-coated wood, that she always kept in her room for afternoon *"goûtés"*; Tini's lurid *True Love Story* magazines I found there and her recitals of the plots of the movies she had seen on her Thursday *"jours de congés."*

During World War II I received a letter for my birthday. I saved it because of its characteristic blend of courage, materialism, good sense, and sentiment. It was written like all her letters, in an original combination of French and French-English.

"Here we are at your *anniversaire* once again. How the time passes, especially when you are getting old. Seventy years is approaching but I have my health and that is the essential.

"I am remembering all the anniversaries I passed with you and I am asking myself what you are doing. Yes, the years go on and my thoughts often go back to when your *Papa* and *Maman* were engaged. I was very much touch that they were telling me right away. I have been part of your family since before that time. I have a nice remembrance of everyone. I had a beautiful collection of postal cards of all the countries we went to but the Germans took them all. Nevertheless I have the remembrance. I remember many things — your *Maman* used to speak to me of my pension for my old age. 'I don't want you to have to worry when you are old, Thérèse,' she used to say. My dear niece, Alice, and her good Gaston would take care of me. Just the same it's nice to have your own.

"We are all well, *Grâce à Dieu.* Gaston is home now. He has not started to repair the inside of the house due to the fact that you cannot get material, but when it will be

D

possible he will start it. He is in no hurry as the outside is done now, at least we are covered. We eat well enough. We do not suffer like the people of the city. All the same we ask each other when this terrible war will be finished.

"Not long ago I had a little accident, *pas grande chose*. I was returning home with the ration when I was struck. *Grâce à Dieu,* I was carrying my wallet, WELL-FILLED inside my *chemise* and the bullet was stopped, taking only a little piece of stomach. I was in the hospital in Belfort for two weeks. Now I am home again since a month and my health is good.

"Remember me kindly to your *Papa, votre frère,* your cousins Marian and Manfred. What good times we all had together. I will always think of the family Frank with a full heart and gratitude. Salutations to *M. votre Mari.* May you all keep safe. If you have a picture of your baby, please send it to me. How he must be big now! I remember when you were born and I lined a wash basket with pink silk because you arrived ahead of time and we were not ready. You were so small! How the years pass!

"Accept, *ma bien chère,* my very best *félicitations* on this occasion, also on the part of Alice and Gaston. May the next year bring you what your heart desires. *Je reste toujours votre bien affectionée,*

Tini

Thérèse Garraud, Champagney, Haute-Saône — France"

The story of Tini's last years (she lived to be ninety-one and her retirement lasted twenty-three years) sounds like a Balzac novel, composed of all the tough, touching, sordid, tragic elements of lower-middle-class French life. The letters kept coming but they grew less cheerful. She had loved her niece as her last blood tie, but it became apparent that her love was not shared and it degenerated into a tyranny founded on the money she had contributed to the household through the years. More and more often she suggested we meet in Paris on one of my trips to Europe. "It would be like the old days with *M.* and *Mme.* Frank." But the reunion never took place. Did I recoil before the ghostly responsibility of representing those shadow figures out of the past? At the last minute, did Tini not wish to confirm her regrets? Or was it simply not practical? I do not know. But soon she grew too old to undertake the journey. Then another letter arrived.

"I am no longer living with Alice and Gaston. They have turned me out, after all my good care of them and money spent on their house! I am living in a *pension.* The landlady interests herself in me and the food is passable. I can't walk any more, my veins give me trouble. On good days I sit in the little garden in the rear that looks over the orchard which is bearing a good crop this year. And I dream of my years with your family . . ."

I saw her, the same figure I remembered, in a rocking chair with her feet on a discarded packing case, but her legs are now wrapped in bandages like the burlap coverings around wintering shrubs. She has white hair, has grown from comfortably plump to very heavy, and there is no sewing basket in her lap. Her familiar rough hands are idle. Far away in place and time, the Frank family: Mamma,

Pappa, Fanny, Irene, Rose, Sarah, Emily are still parading through her mind. They keep her company.

After my son's marriage I wrote Tini and enclosed a newspaper clipping of the event for her memorabilia of the family. But I never saw her writing again. This time I received a politely false letter from her niece. "My Aunt passed away on June first. I am told, peacefully. My husband joins me in thanking you for your generosity through the years . . ."

With Tini, the last inhabitant of the house on Sixty-second Street has disappeared. Brown stone, high stoop, back parlor, dark library, busts of Shakespeare and Beethoven, coatrack, rubber plant are part of a mythical land, a way of life that is growing dim. When I attempt to re-create it I have the impression that I am strolling through a formal city park. The grass is guarded by the arches of low iron fences; the trees are old and cast deep shadows over the straight paths. Bronze statues on marble pedestals look down on this orderly imitation of nature and seem to be telling it to keep its place. A stately procession of open carriages moves by; the horses' hooves echo in my ears, the passengers are leaning toward me and I try to decipher their features but they remain unclear. I will not give them the faces of fiction, because I am searching for some sign of my own being in that remote region of time before I was born.

CHAPTER III

IF MY ATAVISTIC RE-CREATIONS OF MY GRAND-parents' lives represent prehistory, my earliest memories of my parents are ancient history. Although my picture of my father is urban, set against the more manicured section of European cities or the streets of his New York, my first recollection of him is pastoral. We are sitting in a field of daisies which rises above me like an ocean. His head surmounts the white-fringed lacy waves of flowers, and although only in his early forties, he is already bald, with a round face and the swarthy skin of a Spaniard. He holds my hand in his surprisingly small well-tended padded one and I feel at home in the great swaying field under the glaring blue summer sky. We are living in our country home in suburban Westchester. Although it was sold when I was six and my family began its holiday wanderings in Europe, punctuated by the Adirondack summers, I recall the geography of "Green Meadows" and each room in the house as though I were still living there. A few years ago I found my way back to it and was appalled at the shrinking process that had taken place. I will not return, my memories are more substantial than reality.

It was a red brick house with white trim and shutters. The front door faced a circular gravel driveway and beyond, the daisy field. The entrance hall seemed immense and cool even on the hottest day and the stairs mounted in a generous curve, interrupted by the landing that had a bench beneath a tall window that lighted the hall in oblique rays like the interior of a church. This window faced the flower garden, itself as enclosed as a room, paved in red brick and surrounded by a brick wall against which hollyhocks grew as high and pointed as cypress trees.

There were certain objects in the house that appeared significant to me: the grandfather clock in the hall, the wooden contraption shaped like legs in my father's dressing room over which his riding boots were stretched and polished, the hexagonal dessert plates used for state occasions that had a different blooming frosty fruit at the bottom of each. Those inanimate mute objects seem to contain a history also, and at the touch of a wand or a magic word, their secret meanings might become explicit.

"Green Meadows," like Ludwigsburg, was hierarchical, and, like the Kupperman Brewery, our position was near the center. Above us, comparable to the King's palace, was the imposing Tudor mansion of our neighbors, the Rothburgs. Beneath us, the stable and the farmer's cottage. Sometimes on summer evenings I can remember my parents, carefully dressed, on their way to dinner on the hilltop with the Rothburgs. In retrospect I realize and am annoyed by the fact that my mother and father felt honored by the invitation, like good tenants in relation to the manor lords. The Rothburgs were an enormously rich, prominent German-Jewish banking family, and in my childhood they represented an aristocracy with which my family mingled but to which they did not quite belong. I remember them as an imposing couple, she with an ample figure and the cold regular features of a Greek statue, he with a hawk's nose and shining black eyes, resembling a sultan from *The Arabian Nights.* Their sons were fully grown and lived in houses on their parents' estate, disporting themselves with games of tennis and practical jokes like the spoiled somewhat degenerate scions of a Royal Family. The grandchildren were about my age and sometimes they descended from the hill, with their nurses, to play around our sandbox and swings. But unlike their parents and grandparents, they had no regal aura and appeared quite ordinary to me.

The stable and the farmer's cottage were reached by a cinder path. On the way, you passed a chicken coop where garrulous hens, their progeny, and red-crowned roosters were imprisoned by a wire mesh fence in a sandy territory. The chickens scratched and cackled, oblivious of their impending hatchet doom at the hand of the farmer. I averted my eyes but the squalid smell of the coop was not to be avoided. The farmer lived in a compound composed of cottage, stable, barn, and toolshed surrounding a square of grass with a well in the center like a village green. This was another world, seemingly miles away from our house, and I visited it as a foreigner. Wotan, my father's big chestnut horse, was the sole emissary from our kingdom. He had been named, I imagine, not so much to commemorate Wagner's opera or its god-protagonist — although his proportions seemed supernatural to me — but as a sentimental gesture to the brewery in Brooklyn where my father had his roots. Early each morning Wotan would be led to the mounting block in front of our house and my father, scrubbed and elegant, in shining high boots, buff breeches, with a crop tucked under his arm, would ride off, savoring his solitary canter in suburban Westchester as much as the more sociable riding of his youth in Central Park or the Bois de Bologne.

When I was a child, I was my father's companion on his urban rambles in different parts of the world. London, Milan, Vienna, Paris were familiar to him and I was at ease at his side. We would stroll down the vaulted galleries of the Louvre: "This was the home, later the prison of Louis XVI and Marie Antoinette," or in Vienna, "here is where Empress Elizabeth went riding every morning." My father derived pleasure from monumental palaces. Being an engineer, perhaps he divined their hidden skeletons, utilitarian substructures clothed by history with regal lapidary robes and diadems. He was nourished by thoughts of kingly life, and as we walked in the formal maze of the Tuileries Gardens, his steps rang out smartly on the tended gravel paths and he held his small compact person erect.

In New York, while palaces were lacking, the echoing chambers of the Metropolitan Museum and the mansions of the rich (often abandoned, converted, or on the verge of demolition) took their place. To my ears, the names of Astor, Twombley, or Vanderbilt had the ring of royal titles. "They certainly knew how to build in those days," my father would comment. And his pleasure in solid achievement outweighed the melancholy that might have been induced by the buildings' desertion and ultimate destruction.

But my favorite walk was one we rarely took. It led us toward Central Park South, west to where there is an apartment building, still standing, elaborately carved with gargoyles. This was the scene of my father's bachelor years, a time that seemed unbelievable to me. He lived here with two other legendary bachelors, a cousin, since grown crotchety and forlorn, and a handsome bearded photographer, now world famous. It was difficult for me to picture my comfortable domesticated father as a dashing man about town. I had seen a photograph of him from that period — a class picture when he graduated from Columbia's School of Mines (that name, too, had an improbable ring, glittering as though surrounded by diamonds, but I learned later that all it actually meant was that my father had chosen to break with family tradition and become an engineer instead of a brewer like his older brother). On that photograph, my father's ears stuck out from his head and his face looked unnaturally thin, unlike the chubby one I was used to, with its broad elfin nose and small brown-green eyes with their depths of humor and understanding. Also, he had a heavy shock of black hair, while as long as I knew him, he had been almost bald, having lost his hair in a bout of typhoid fever in Paris, contracted from eating a contaminated oyster. The likeness is far from a romantic one, yet I was fascinated by tales of my father's life at that time. They were told to me by friends and relatives, as he was always silent about personal matters from the past, likely to say, "How you talk!" or, "I don't remember," if reminded of them. But my mother and I both loved to hear details about his early successes in a glamorous world of actresses and famous beauties, as though they were decorations he had received in foreign wars. I pictured after-theater suppers with pink-shaded lamps, sky-blue jewelers' boxes, and long-stemmed American Beauty roses. But unlike Cousin David's spending, my father's was tinged with practicality. It brought pleasure to him and the lady concerned, but he did not delude himself that she was a misunderstood saint, nor did he ever dream of marrying her. Some day he would marry, but it would be "suitable" as well as romantic. Whether my father realized it at the time or not, he partook of the Kuppermans' solid conventional bourgeois attitude.

My father dropped everyone from his bachelor life, like an entertaining novel never to be reread, when he finally married my mother at the ripe age of forty. But many years later, in a restaurant, I spotted a famous actress from that era at a table adjoining the one where my father, then eighty, my husband, and I were seated. She had retained the remains of her former prettiness, with a tip-tilted nose, soft white powdered papery skin, and piles of tinted hair that one could see had once been golden. She was wearing an Edwardian pearl and diamond dog collar and her whole costume had an elaborate femininity not to be found in the little black dresses of the day. Suddenly, surprisingly, she leaned toward my father, touching his shoulder with her little beringed age-spotted hand: "Arthur!" she exclaimed, "after all these years!" And then she added with genuine solicitude, "But, oh my dear, I'm afraid you haven't been taking care of yourself."

Both my parents have told me of their meeting at the home of a mutual friend. My mother was then almost thirty, having whiled away long dreary years in her family's house of mourning. There had been an engagement ten years earlier that she had broken, having mistaken intellectual compatibility for love, and then a coming together again at what she had known was her fiancé's deathbed from tuberculosis. My mother's youth had been as somber as my father's had been colorful, and yet she was by nature gay and gregarious, but with a lurking shadow of fear and pessimism, while my father, at least in later years, was unvivacious and inarticulate in comparison to her. But he had profound reserves of optimism and an unquenchable joy of living. Perhaps this opposition was an asset in their twenty-odd years of marriage. And perhaps some instinct of this prompted my father when he fell in love with her at first sight. At any rate, she was outwardly all he could desire: blond, beautiful in a flawless fashion — everything he required of women — and she came from a correct family. When he saw her at that first meeting, dressed all in white like an angel, he determined to marry her. The next day, she related, he took her for a drive in Central Park. My mother liked to tell how when they started out she had regarded him as a rather homely man, nervous and uncertain, with sweating palms. It is strange that my father, so successful and experienced with women, could have, at first, been frightened by my mother. What happened, what was said on that short ride I was not told or, perhaps, the details are unimportant, because the imagination of love is unpredictable and not to be explained, and it can make marble halls out of sticks and stones. It is directed by some power outside the individual, maybe in accordance with nature by some preordained plan that is hidden in the commonplace everyday. And we respond unwittingly, like sleepwalkers. At any rate, my mother returned from the drive in Central Park in love for the first time — and last — I believe. And I am certain that in her presence my father's hands were never again damp from nervousness and uncertainty.

In a sense, this was my beginning. And because the story of my parents' courtship is so familiar to me, it seems incongruous that I was absent, not even thought of at that time. Also it is somewhat frightening and lonely to realize that so much was happening, for so long, without my being there.

My father's life was divided into separate islands: his German upbringing within the walls of the brewery in Brooklyn, his bachelor days, the contented enclosed time of his marriage, and then almost twenty years again of return to bachelorhood after my mother's death. It seems to me that when I was a child, he had turned his back on his early days, he was a dutiful son and a devoted brother, but his visits at the brewery were rare and unofficial and his interests were located in his engineering firm. I remember his partner, Walter Keogh, a noisy giant Irishman, who would blow in for dinner, blasting us with his raucous laughter and enthusiasm for the bridges, railways, and tunnels he and my father were constructing. My father would often make precise drawings for my amusement of converging rails or bridge suspensions, and without understanding it, I looked on his and Mr. Keogh's achievements as nothing short of miraculous. In the late twenties, the brewery faded. It was the Prohibition era and sometimes my father would return from his weekly visit to his brother in Brooklyn with an odd medley of objects manufactured at the brewery to keep the machinery in motion. I can remember that they produced rubber pants, which I used on my dolls, cocoa, and something called "near beer," which I never beheld, but the name had a pinched dismal sound, reminding me of the frozen-nosed army of unemployed selling apples on the street corners during those Depression years. Because of my youth and because my father, I do not know how, escaped the effect of that black time, Prohibition and the Crash meant no more to me than rubber pants and those patient apple vendors on the streets of New York. All of it is now history and although I was there, I did not participate in it, and it is as strange to me as the Battle of Waterloo or the Civil War.

During those years after my grandfather's death, it was Uncle Carl who continued the Kupperman tradition. My earliest recollection finds him in his house in Brooklyn (facing Prospect Park), where I was an infrequent visitor. I hated the big brick house, most of all the perfectly equipped gymnasium at the top and Aunt Terry, who was ubiquitous and domineering. Her shining black eyes seemed to be multiplied by her quivering pince-nez as she exhorted her children to ever-greater daring on the rings, ropes, and ladders of the gymnasium, while I, an inept outsider, hoped in vain that her four darting eyes would overlook me. "Who is a coward?" she would jeer and the ugly question seemed to include Uncle Carl. With his old-fashioned beard and watery blue eyes, he resembled a faded Santa Claus, a gentler reproduction of his father. He was no match for Aunt Terry's demonic energy and he would look at her with apologetic doglike devotion and admiration.

There was an unspoken tragedy in the house in Brooklyn. It revolved around the oldest son, Paul, who spoke explosively and moved spasmodically. He couldn't learn to ride a bicycle like the other children who careened around the gravel path at the back of the house, with Aunt Terry wildly shouting, "Faster faster!" It was years before I realized, from bits of overheard conversation, that he was "different." His gawky presence haunted the house in Brooklyn, adding to its gloom.

Family legend recounted the courtship of Uncle Carl and Aunt Terry in the German-American brewing circle of Brooklyn. It was a good solid match; "Old Man" Bruchner owned a comparable brewery and his wealth equaled the Kuppermans'. Although Adolph Bruchner died before my birth, tales of him persisted. By the time they reached me, they had an improbable ring, but legend must be swallowed whole or not at all. He appeared to me a towering man with a booming voice and a thick German accent. He had had a surprisingly indigenous American boyhood. His parents were pioneers in the covered wagon days and it was said that young Adolph had himself dug the graves for several sisters and brothers and for his own mother, on the stern move westward. But the Bruchners were of hardy prolific stock and many survived. The eventual termination of the rugged journey in a Brooklyn brewery courtyard remained a miracle to me, but I accepted it as I did the transformation of the bear into hero in the fairytales of my childhood. In my imagination, Adolph Bruchner emerged as a composite Abraham Lincoln-Kaiser-Captain Hook.

Aunt Terry never allowed us to forget her pioneering forebears or ceased to press the point that she, Marie Theresa Bruchner, the fifth daughter of the nine sons and daughters of Adolph Bruchner, had for love of Uncle Carl consented to marry a Jew. "My poor children," she would lament in my presence, "you will not have the advantages of your Bruchner cousins because your father is Jewish." In spite of the closeness and homogeneity of the German-American brewing families of her day, Aunt Terry always made it sound as though through some largess of her own spirit, she had chosen to marry a creature from another planet.

Later she and Uncle Carl moved from the house near Prospect Park to a Fifth Avenue apartment. My cousins, older than I, were by then dispersed, married, at college, or traveling. Paul had also vanished, to an institution I heard later. And although the apartment had rooms for everyone, I remember Uncle Carl and Aunt Terry, at this time, chiefly alone. She would alternate sighs for her tragedy and great love with gusty returns of boisterous activity. I was thankful that the detested gymnasium and the brick-paved garden were no more, and in her captivity, perched high above Central Park, Aunt Terry reminded me of a crow in a cage. I often studied her portrait over the mantelpiece and marveled that this handsome girl draped in a pale pink feather boa could be the seamed, gray woman I knew.

Uncle Carl stood for the continuation of family tradition, and at times patient endurance can pass for strength. His beard and blandly jovial manner were becoming to a patriarch. "Hello, Polly girl," he would greet me, pinching my cheek but avoiding my eye. On my visits to the brewery, he seemed a proper chief. Still faintly Germanic in style, he never looked so authoritative as when he held a full stein of beer to the light, appraising its golden color and white crown, and then drank slowly, thoughtfully wiping the foam from his lip, which looked like a ripe fruit in the foliage of his sandy beard. Next to the blondness of Uncle Carl, my father, smooth-shaven and dark, looked as though he had sprung from a different source. Uncle Carl was slow and deliberate, my father quick and impatient. Their differences made them alien to one another, but loving. A disparate tandem, they were linked together by the ties of family feeling through all the years of their long lives.

Uncle Carl continued to go to the brewery each day of his existence until his death at the age of ninety. When he sat at the lunch table in the house that had been the office of his grandfather and his father, under the portraits of his ancestors, his appearance mirrored theirs. He seemed to be preserving himself by absorbing the past, through an elixir of beer, in an atmosphere redolent with the meaty smell of malt.

In my childhood, traces of the old Kupperman way of life remained. High up in our New York City apartment, touches of Christmas as it had been observed in Ludwigsburg and in the three homes in the brewery yard persisted. My father, having inherited his atheism from his father and grandfather, ignored the Jewish holidays. But for him, Christmas was not a Christian holiday either, rather it was a time to celebrate the reoccurrence of warm family ritual.

In my memory, childhood Christmases are always white. The snow made its appearance in advance, like a backdrop curtain that is lowered before the play begins. And I do not remember the commercial colored lights, hideous Santa Clauses, reindeer, and mannequin angels in front of the department stores that now make a travesty of the holiday in the autumn when the city may still be blanketed by the lingering tepid aftermath of summer.

When I was a child, Christmas did not approach slowly, candidly in the open, but burst in full force on the afternoon leading up to Christmas Eve when Mademoiselle and I would be sent out into the snowy streets under a gunmetal sky that was as supercharged as the electric atmosphere before a summer's thunderstorm. For some unknown reason, part of the unvarying ritual, we always walked toward Madison Avenue to visit Mademoiselle's friend and compatriot, Julia Nicolier, the dry cleaner. Since I rarely visited this establishment except on Christmas Eve, it too seemed loaded with excitement, and Madame Nicolier herself, with her neat bun of hair and her cheeks which from a distance looked rosy, but on closer inspection were lined with tiny crisscrossed red veins like the rivers on a map, appeared a lovely Annunciation Angel. The smell of steam and dampened cloth in the shop were as delicious as spice and frankincense.

When we returned home the streets were dark and the lamps already lit. Inside our apartment the living room doors were tightly shut and the fact that I knew exactly the spectacle that would greet me when they opened never lessened my impatience. At six o'clock, my mother at the piano began to play "Silent Night" and the doors opened on what seemed to be the same giant tree that made its appearance each Christmas Eve. It reached to the ceiling with a silver star at its peak. It was bedecked in all the bright sticky-looking ornaments that had survived the years (perhaps some were left from the Brooklyn Christmases), garlanded in tinsel and lit by as many candles as there are stars in a summer sky. Tini, our French maid, who had been with my family as long as some of the decorations on the tree and with much more usefulness to us all, stood with a pail of water to douse the candles in case of fire. Beneath the tree in tempting variously shaped gaily wrapped bundles the presents waited on a spread sheet (to catch the pine needles), not to be opened until the last carol had been sung. The pleasant agony of anticipation was accompanied by the singing of "O Tannenbaum" and "Adeste Fidelis" and the intoxicating smell of pine and dripping wax. The room always seemed crowded but I am not sure of the cast of characters, as everything was in darkness except for the lighted tree. Besides my parents and brother, there must have been the ubiquitous Mademoiselle, the cook, and the parlor maid, changing from year to year, and perhaps an assortment of familyless relatives and acquaintances whose faces have become blank with time. When my mother finally shut the piano, candles were extinguished and the electric lights switched on, but my brother and I, in accordance with ritual, were forced to wait while the packages were handed out to the circle of servants and hangers-on, in feudal fashion, in attenuated imitation of the days when the Kuppermans had gathered in huge family conclave. At last the signal was given and my brother and I rushed upon our presents like ravening wolves. In no time the gaudy wrapping paper was torn away and the presents strewn about in a scene of devastation. Nothing remained of the once decorous setting, so full of promise, except the tree, aloof and beautiful but now forgotten. Its moment of supreme rule was over for another year. Sometimes I felt a stab of sadness only mitigated by the promise of the Christmas stocking, nubbly with miniature presents, marzipan fruits from Germantown, and strings of black corrugated licorice called shoelaces that my father loved from his childhood. I secretly loathed them but managed to conceal it from him and chewed them dutifully, trying to mimic his enthusiasm. When I awoke early on Christmas morning, the deformed silhouette of the overflowing stocking would greet me in vague outline in the dark. It was topped by a sprig of holly and it reassured me that the excitement of Christmas Eve, so long awaited, so quickly over, did have its morning postscript, delightful too, a pure concoction of Santa Claus without the awesome echoes of "Silent Night" and, for me, the veiled and mysterious significance of Christmas Eve.

Why is it so difficult to recall the faces of those closest to us? They must be teased into being by bringing back their environment, streets, houses, rooms, furniture, the lesser characters surrounding them, the seasons and special days returning with regularity, such as Christmas, anniversaries, birthdays. These dates are the punctuation marks in the undifferentiated passing of time.

Birthdays were important in our family. In retrospect, my parents' birthdays appear like abstract portraits of them. July 20, my father's, full summer, was a bold season marked by travel and a certain restlessness. March 12, my mother's date, always found us at home. Treacherous winds, piles of melted snow at the street crossings, and bare buffeted branches in the park proclaimed winter's grip. But the lengthening days, the appearance of anemones and carnations in the florists' windows suggested the fragility of returning spring.

We were often in Europe when my father's birthday came around again — in one of those European cities he enjoyed so much. My brother and I would shop in secret: a tie bought under the arcade of the Rue de Rivoli, a wooden cuckoo clock found up the steep alley of a Swiss village, the black- and silver-checked penknife, purchased I no longer remember where, that my father wore on his watch chain to the day he died. He would be breakfasting upstairs in our hotel suite when we made our presentation. His newly shaved brown cheeks felt smooth and smelled of soap when I kissed him. He was enjoying his ample uncontinental breakfast with gusto, his napkin tucked inside his vest, eating stewed prunes and drinking coffee a little noisily while reading the European edition of the *Herald Tribune*. Over his shoulder I could see a view of Alpine range, tree-bordered boulevard, narrow ancient street. Most likely we had arrived late the night before, grimy from the train, into a strange dark world, and my morning impressions of a new place were confused and tentative. But with my father's familiar silhouette in the foreground, the view from the window was beckoning and I was eager to go outside.

Sometimes he would stop in front of a *pâtisserie* and the savory perfume of fresh baking reached us as my brother and I looked into the window where tarts and fancy bread were displayed like edible jewels. "Select one," my father commanded. After long deliberation, my brother would choose a bursting chocolate eclair and I, a billowing brioche with a glazed golden-brown dome. "Good! Now you have had enough," my father would exclaim and we would move on, leaving the eclair and the brioche in their untouched, untasted beauty behind us. I'm sure there must have been protests, but this bad joke of my father's, often repeated, has not left a bad memory. It remains part of his reassuring presence, part of summer mornings in new places, connected, in some way, with those July birthdays that help me to recall my father's face.

For weeks in advance of my mother's birthday, each afternoon I would be preparing her present, embroidering a cushion or a towel supervised by Mademoiselle. I see her with a clarity that is denied my mother's image — a tall woman of indeterminate middle age with a frizzy bang and a red throat and chest on which a small diamond pendant rested like the evening star in a ruddy sunset. When she was agitated, this color heightened to vermilion and was the precursor to one of her migraine headaches. While I sewed clumsily, she would read to me from one of the books of the *Bibliothèque rose,* quaint moralistic tales by the Comtesse de Ségur. The everyday happenings of those little French children seemed as fantastic and grotesque as fairytales. I loved the set with its deep pink covers embossed in gold and the black and white illustrations showing children with old faces and in elaborate clothes being perpetually admonished by their elders, parents, and guardians, in similar costumes with the same faces — to be distinguished from their charges by size alone.

Sometimes Mademoiselle would tell me stories about her own aunt, who had been governess to the ill-fated Romanovs before the Russian Revolution. In my mind's eye, those children also had old sad faces and their tragic fate was confused in my imagination with the minor mishaps of *Les Malheurs de Sophie.* A small enameled Russian easter egg, a present from her aunt, attested to the truth of Mademoiselle's stories and gave her for me a certain prestige.

As March 12 drew near, it usually happened that I was behind schedule. Mademoiselle had to finish the pillow slip, and so some of the roses, blooming in uneven lumpy stitching, were mine, while others, executed with the faultless precision of a machine, were hers.

My mother never appeared to notice this contrast. I can see her on the birthday morning, sitting up in bed, her long fair hair held back by a velvet ribbon, receiving, with ever-renewed surprise and joy, the birthday offering. Although the cushions multiplied on her chaise longue and the cross-stitched towels in her bathroom, it seems to me now that she appreciated even more the last-minute poem or crayon drawing I had hurriedly created the night before, vaguely sensing that my mother would be reminded of Mademoiselle every time she looked at her birthday gift and that I would be overshadowed, just as my mother's lovely sensitive appearance is now, at times, overpowered by the memory of Mademoiselle's ruddy, frizzled, well-corseted image.

If Mademoiselle's unwelcome likeness sometimes obstructs my early recollections of my mother, Cousin Irene, though seen infrequently, composes in my mind a double image with her. I often looked at their bridal photographs. Aunt and niece, eight years apart, were married within six months of one another. In their pictures they are wearing similar satin dresses, veils and wreaths on their long fair hair, worn in the puffy pompadour fashionable at that time. They somewhat resembled each other and the differences between them served to highlight each. My mother in her modish wedding costume looks unworldly, with a faraway gaze in her wide-set eyes, as though a helpless seraphic being had descended to this planet to be draped, molded, and fitted by a stylish dressmaker. Cousin Irene, on the contrary, seems at home in her satin and tulle; fashion becomes her and soft expensive fabrics were as much a part of her as her well-tended skin. Although so different in many ways, my mother and Irene, separated by a continent (Irene lived in San Francisco after her marriage), maintained a close enthusiastic friendship, begun long ago in the house on Sixty-second Street when Emily and young Irene sought the solace of each other's company in the midst of the Frank family's gloomy seclusion. When Cousin Irene came to visit us when I was a child, my mother's spirits would rise miraculously. I would observe Irene, admiring her latest costume from Paris, the Grecian symmetry of her body, and her perfect poise. But I often heard her and my mother laughing together, sounding like young girls sharing some private joke.

Sometimes when we did not go abroad, my family would visit Irene on the West Coast. I remember those times and that place with perfect clarity. There are people who use their homes as accessories, playgrounds, laboratories, or stages. But the home of Cousin Irene also seemed to be part of her very person, a tranquil and beautiful outgrowth of her fastidious aristocratic nature. Even the heavy summer garden smells blended with the special perfume she always wore.

Along the drive from San Francisco the countryside looked parched. The road was flanked by bare yellow ocher hills, but as you approached the house, rows of tall eucalyptus trees with shaggy peeling bark and sparse foliage came forward to meet you. They reminded me of a caravan of molting camels. In the summer breeze they gave off an aroma of Oriental spice. As you turned into the driveway, there was a sudden cool shock of emerald-green lawns, constantly freshened by festoons of sprinklers. Here was an oasis. You had arrived at Burlingame.

The house itself was almost indistinguishable, smothered by vines outside and filled inside with huge basins of heavy creamy peonies. Irene would move slowly to meet you, with the still grace of a swan. She was impeccable in white and had an aureole of golden hair and moonlit skin that looked as though it had always been shielded from any rougher element than the fragrant atmosphere of her home. She had a slightly clouded luminosity like an opal.

I remember the early mornings in Burlingame most clearly. Some summers my parents and I lived in the "bungalow" and sometimes I spent the vacation with my cousins Marian and Manfred in the "big house." At the bungalow, I woke to a golden day. In the gilt-papered dining area, Perfeto Amor, the Philippine houseboy, would be setting out fresh figs and cream on the breakfast table. Through the window near my bed I could often see Manfred (long-legged in patched corduroys and a sloppy shirt that did not succeed in disguising his angelic beauty), sailing his boat in the lily pond. The dew on the brilliant green lawn was a net of diamonds. In the big house I shared a sleeping porch with Marian, and the nights and early mornings were wine-fresh and redolent of eucalyptus.

Cousin Irene always remained in the pink and green bower of her bedroom until late morning. But although she was in retirement, we were all aware that the smooth running of the entire house went according to her plan. In the evenings she bloomed. I was an avid spectator of her entrance into the living room, where, with her children and husband, I awaited her. She would float down the stairs in pale diaphanous tea gowns, trailing chiffon wings and train. And with her always came the enveloping whiff of perfume. At the dinner table Irene's voice was gentle, but it dominated Marian's noisy chatter. Her husband at the other end of the table took all his cues from her. His somewhat average appearance and personality seemed to take on importance and reassurance from her regality. She always placed Manfred, her youngest, next to her, as though his golden beauty was bound to hers by an invisible integument.

These California visits punctuated my childhood and marked the transitions of my growing up. Marian, two years older than I, was for a long time a step ahead of me in experience. I had been there when she returned from camp, hair matted and grimy, but glorious with athletic emblems and trophies. "For heaven's sake, disinfect her before she comes downstairs for dinner," Irene would order with good-natured disgust, wrinkling her sensitive nose with its narrow transparent nostrils that were lined in pale pink like the inside of a shell. A season or two later I watched enviously as Marian turned from a muscular hoyden into a pert young girl with light-brown braids wound around her head and new small breasts that looked enormous to me.

When I was fourteen, there was a family gathering to decide whether I was old enough to be included in a costume dance to which Marian was going. Until then I had been a mere observer of the adult world. Love and sex meant remote crushes on actors and musical virtuosos and reading Viña Delmar's *Bad Girl* (forbidden fare), curled up luxuriously on a sofa with a fresh slice of coconut layer cake.

The night of the party I felt uncertain and elated. But I actively disliked my blue-checked gingham dress and poke bonnet. I was costumed to be a baby and I feared it was a meager disguise! I looked admiringly at Marian, representing the young Madame de Pompadour, in a *robe de style*, with her hair piled high and a coquettish black beauty spot on her cheek.

I remember almost nothing about the party (except that it was held outdoors near a swimming pool), until the moment when a masterful figure, dressed as a pirate, cut in on my partner. The pirate and I moved off to sit in a hammock on the edge of the dance floor in the latticed glow of tree lights. He was self-confident and I soon learned had reached the admirable age of twenty. In his dark eyes I saw something I had never seen before — open admiration of me. My unease was melting away, but I prayed silently he would never discover I was only fourteen. As he talked, he twirled a toy dagger, aiming it playfully at my heart. But when it was time to leave, suddenly serious, he grasped my wrists and kissed me. The kiss surprised me as much as an earth tremor and was scarcely more enjoyable. "When will I see you again?" he asked. I neither knew the answer, nor did I much care. At that moment I felt quite complete and eager to be alone, to savor my newly found power.

After that my observations of Irene took a different form.

I still admired her goddess proportions, but my admiration was no longer disinterested. I had been a clear pool, recording the reflection of a lush garden; I became a mirror, in which my surroundings were a background for my own image. When we were alone, Marian and I would imitate Irene's walk; we even, surreptitiously, tried on her tea gowns, but found the wings and trains too much to manage. Most of all, I wanted to have her perfume, *Whisper of Venus*, follow me as it did her. But although I dabbed it generously behind my ears, I lost the scent as soon as it was on me.

Cousin Irene and my mother are both dead and the house and bungalow and garden have been sold to make a public park. I have never gone back, but I can imagine the desecration. The lawn is spotted by those instruments of torture now found in children's playgrounds: severed culverts, jungles of iron mazes, ladders, rings, and bars. The lily pond is choked and neglected and surrounded by peanut husks and Popsicle sticks. The bungalow has been converted into a lavatory and the big house — the fate of the big house is hazy. It has either been razed or it stands closed and empty like those giant crustaceans washed up by the sea, whose shells remain intact from primeval times, but whose inhabitants have long ago been devoured by preying animals.

My memories of Burlingame are so distant that they no longer seem to be founded on fact. Also I have come to doubt that there ever was a woman called Irene; a golden opalescent work of art stands in her place. In recent years, upon my occasional meetings with Marian and Manfred, I am always startled to find that they have a share in my familiar dream. But not long ago in a crowded store, I caught the scent of *Whisper of Venus* and the present dissolved. I was back again in the emerald oasis, festooned with sprinklers, back in the long-abandoned house, where the creamy peonies drooped their heavy heads and shed their petals in the plenitude of summer.

Those visits in Burlingame were entered through the doll's house door of the bungalow or the vine-hung entrance of the big house. The threshold of my European summers was the raised iron partition to be stepped over at the end of the steep gangplank as I boarded an ocean liner. My feelings were mixed when I crossed this threshold, compounded of regret at leaving my friends and familiar places and the pounding excitement caused by the prospect of new sights that always seized me as the ship's great horn blasted, "All visitors ashore," and the shouting, waving figures on the pier grew jumbled and dim as we steamed out of the harbor.

I often think of these departures now when I leave for Europe by plane. The airport is as antiseptic as a hospital, the crossing speedy, accompanied by the matter-of-fact monotonous drone of jet engines and the bland, efficient ministrations of the stewardesses, so like hospital nurses. When we are put down at a foreign airport, it is identical to the one we have just left, the same antiseptic atmosphere, the same expressionless loudspeaker voice announcing arrivals and departures in several languages, all of them vaguely incorrect like an instrument that is always off key. And one steps out on to foreign soil as from a hygienic cocoon — abruptly without transition, as unprepared for travel as a patient dismissed from the unnatural confines of a hospital.

How different were the Atlantic crossings of my childhood, protracted hyphens of changing seas between the United States and Europe. The ship was a continent in itself composed of various states. There was the promenade deck where the hours were counted by consommé and saltines served at noon and tea and gingersnaps at five o'clock. Here the inhabitants of the floating world stretched out on deck chairs and covered themselves with plaid blankets, or walked briskly but pointlessly around and around. In my memory all the women are wearing white flannel skirts and white felt slouch hats and the men are dressed in tweed knickers and peaked golf caps. It was here that one was trapped, "to get a little fresh air," when the seas were stormy and one felt too queasy to leave the deck chair and flee to the longed-for privacy of the cabin. At these times the rising and falling miles between deck and cabin seemed endless and untraversable and one remained glued to the spot, helplessly watching the heaving gray foam-flecked sea sinking and climbing outside the salt-sprayed glass panes of the promenade deck. My father was never seasick and on the stormiest day would appear happy and healthy in his plus fours and bow tie, urging the rest of us unfeelingly to join him in a long dangerous meal in the gilded dining room below, or a sickening movie in the potted palm jungle of the lounge.

Soon after we left the shore behind us, my father would secure a passenger list to study the names of our fellow floating citizens, their offspring and vassals. I was glad when there were large families and I would have other children to share this world between worlds with me. Otherwise I was obliged to follow listlessly behind my parents, passing the long days watching other people enjoying themselves, dancing in the evening to sentimental tunes never meant for me, or fighting with my brother over a game of shuffleboard or ring tennis on the sports deck. Sometimes there would be a famous actor or actress on board. Those would be the best crossings, and evading Mademoiselle and my family, I would follow him or her with the persistence of a private detective — staring and admiring, falling in love from a safe distance, and trying to reconstruct this glamorous life coinciding with mine for the duration of an Atlantic crossing.

By the last day my cabin had become home, the damp salt smell part of my own skin and hair, and the uninterrupted view of sea and sky beyond my porthole was as accustomed as Park Avenue's busy canyon outside my bedroom window in New York. At this point land would be sighted. All the white-skirted, knickerbockered passengers would crowd forward on the deck to get a first glimpse of the shore, no more than a fuzzy irregularity on the horizon. They were as excited as a crowd of early explorers and as the coast of France or England grew clearer and the shapes of houses, tiny as a toy village, could be discerned, the sight was heady, like the vision of an unchartered land bristling with savages and wild animals. We had arrived. And as I again stepped over the raised iron threshold and began to descend the gangplank, my excitement returned, with regret at leaving home — this time, the well-known continent of the big ship that had faithfully, with so many protesting groans and creakings, carried me across the sea.

It was across the iron threshold of a ship that my mother stepped on the day I saw her for the last time. Like so many turning points in my life, I did not recognize it at the moment. How often do we round a corner unaware of its portentousness and of the new atmosphere we are about to enter? How is it possible, we ask ourselves afterward, that there were no signs or signals on the road to indicate the direction toward which we were being carried? On this day, after my wedding, when I was twenty-one, the present was absorbing me completely. The future, if I was aware of it at all, involved no one but myself and this intimate stranger to whom I had been married the day before. Therefore, I barely noticed my mother and father when they came to see us off. Now from the distance of so many years, I glimpse my mother dimly, a diminished figure seen through the wrong end of a telescope, dressed in a dowdy summer print with a shapeless straw hat, a tired, crumpled appearance, but with that incandescent beauty always shining through like a glow of light behind a shabby lampshade. I do not remember her words because I did not know that they would be the last she would address to me, and when the ship's horn sounded, I was relieved to see my parents disembark toward the anonymous crowd on the pier. This time the blast did not make my heart pound at the promise of new places, but at the prospect of being alone again with this exciting still incompletely explored human being who was called my husband, and whose name I was now proudly bearing like a dazzling shield. I remember my parents turning to wave as they descended the gangplank. But I moved away before they had disappeared below, unaware that my mother had vanished from my life forever.

Now I realize that I knew her at the wrong age. Not long ago an evening at Carnegie Hall led me to this reflection. I entered the auditorium (after my temporary defection to the new Concert Hall) with a grateful feeling of homecoming. Here there were no bright metals and furry plush or ramps and glass walls, only vaulted space to harbor the ghosts of bygone audiences. As I sat at the front of the box listening to the nostalgic chirps of the violins tuning up, these phantom music lovers hovered around me, enriching the air with their invisible presences. Chief among them was my mother. Her response to music, unshared and resented in my childhood, had communicated itself to me in later years like a beneficent legacy. As I leaned over the worn railing of the box, looking down into the orchestra's abstract pattern of white shirt fronts, black coats, and golden-brown instruments, I knew the moment of anticipation my mother had experienced so many times while I sat sullenly by her side. This night we were to hear Verdi's *Requiem*. As the chorus filed in (the women in motley dress and hair styles, the soloists spangled and gross), it was hard to believe that in a few seconds they would fuse, their fussy individual façades melting in mighty unison into one magic instrument of musical flight.

In my childhood the performances of the Touroff Choir

were a source of acute embarrassment to me. Not only was the conductor, Marguerita Touroff, a woman — a freakish fact — but my own mother was part of the ill-assorted group that formed the chorus. As I watched her troop on stage, I used to hope she would be unrecognizable, but I always spotted her at once, looking both indecently familiar and shockingly strange, like an unexpected encounter with one's own reflection in a mirror. Madame Touroff, a spinster, was invariably dressed in dusty black as though ever ready to step out onto the podium. But she appeared most distasteful to me when she visited us at home. She had gray hair dressed high on her head in stiff waves like corrugated metal, a red face with strong mannish features, and bulging blue eyes. Her foreign accent was as ungainly as her bony body and gnarled hands. There were two incongruities in connection with Marguerita Touroff: one was that my mother should be so pleased to welcome her, and the other was Madame Touroff's chair which stood in our living room. Fragile and ornate with bowed carved legs and covered in flowered silk, it should have belonged to a French king's favorite. Certainly it had no affinity with Madame Touroff or with our somber living room and its heavy furniture. It was always referred to as "Madame Touroff's chair," and it outlasted her regular appearances for dinner and survived my mother by many years. Only after my father's death was it sold to a second-hand furniture dealer. I wonder who has inherited it now.

Across the dinner table I would jealously watch my mother's face light up with interest as she and Madame

Touroff discussed the program for a forthcoming concert. My mother's face was mobile and transparent, with a beauty that was too familiar for appreciation. It had the pale perfection of English bone china and her moods shone through with great clarity. There was the expression of panic when there was even the slightest illness in the family, the uncertain conscientious look when she would be ordering from the grocer according to the cook's list: "one head of Simpson lettuce, five pounds of granulated sugar, two cans of Old Dutch cleanser" — like a schoolgirl who has memorized her lesson but has not understood it. Running a house was difficult for her, but for that very reason, in accordance with her scrupulousness, she forced herself awkwardly to attend to its myriad small duties. My mother could often escape into the brilliant gaiety of those who are by nature melancholy. At those times her conversation was electric, her laughter contagious. But the kind of rapt attention she gave to the subject of the Touroff Choir was unwelcome to me — perhaps because I secretly longed for some participation in that world of music I always pretended to scorn.

On the stage at Carnegie Hall the orchestra, chorus, and soloists had opened the *Requiem*. "Grant them rest eternal, Lord, and let perpetual light shine upon them —" Here was a prayer for the dead, yet its effect was rousing, at once solemn and intoxicating. With the aid of music it is momentarily possible to embrace all of life, recoiling at nothing, not even death, to reach into the very heart of the world. "Unto Thee all flesh shall come. Lord, have mercy —" I felt a hand from the rear of the box grasp my shoulder and pound my back.

"That means you, too, kid," someone whispered. The surprising words seemed just right at this moment. It did mean me too. And with the music to buoy me, I accepted my common fate with elation. I turned to look at the speaker, a man of late middle years, vigorous and large, with the high balding forehead of a prophet, a heavy jowled face with a Churchillian cast of feature. "That means you, too, kid," he repeated, and his glittering eyes reflected my own excitement. It was as though the box were a ship's prow fronting a gale over a stormy sea toward an unknown destination and only we two were awake in a darkened world, roused by the wonderfully dangerous voyage.

When I was young, the thought of death often haunted me — sometimes in the midst of busy daylight hours I could brush it away with my many small serious projects, but at night, in bed, my defenses were down. Under the attack I would shrink inside my fresh sheets and try to concentrate on a patch of flickering light reflected on the ceiling from the busy city street outside my open window. In vain — the metaphysical jimjam would have to run its course. It began with a kind of mental chant: *Who am I? I am nothing, come from nothing, going to nothing. I might have been a rock, a toad, a blade of grass . . .* Like a witch's incantation, these words had the power to terrify me, to make me lose my bearings utterly. Should I cry out? Should I run to my mother for help? But I never did, because I could see, in advance, her scared white face, gentle with too much understanding. We would be drawn together in the great void of my fancy. Then I would think of my father, "What nonsense," he would say, "don't be an idiot." The mere thought of his ordinary words and careless warmth would reassure me and I would fall asleep at last, the incantation silent, my mother's pale face banished, filled with the comforting idea of my father.

In later years it occurred to me that my father had a similar effect upon my mother. In the eyes of the world it seemed remarkable that so much beauty and rare intellect could be enslaved by this small ugly man. He himself never grew accustomed to his good fortune. Yet he was selfish and demanding, she self-sacrificing and compliant. It was as though my mother lacked a protective epidermis and this my father supplied.

When Hitler came to power in Germany, my mother, far away and protected on these shores, without any connection abroad, took to her bed. "Nervous exhaustion," the doctor said. And as I tiptoed past her door, I vowed I would never be like her — in no way. Since I had not inherited my mother's blond classical beauty but was dark like my father, it seemed possible that my vow would be carried out. "What a shame she doesn't take after her mother!" her friends would sometimes say, little guessing that while I longed to be pretty, I quietly exulted in their tactlessness.

The *Requiem* was coming to a close; with the final "Libera me" the soprano's voice rose in passionate appeal and was overwhelmed by the chorus and orchestra. "Deliver me, Lord, from eternal death . . ." The prayer is both desperate and commanding. In music, the human being standing before death is made over in heroic proportions — awed and glorified. After the tempest of sound, the last notes diminished softly into silence, leaving me bemused and feeling as though eons had passed since the opening of the Mass.

But time is treacherous and paradoxically, the twenty years I lived with my mother seem condensed into a minute. Nothing remains but disconnected images that float into memory as though they were pages from someone else's family album. I see her sitting before the mirror in her bedroom, while Miss Nelly, the hairdresser, who looks like a scarecrow, waves her hair with crimping irons and pins it into an old-fashioned bun. When I return from school she is resting on her couch. Her closed eyes and the blue veins of her temples make her face look as lifeless as marble. Only the long amber necklace she always wears looks alive; each bead holds a tiny orange flame at its center and is warm to the touch. I see her at the piano, her pure profile in silhouette against the window, and hear her modest accurate voice and the slight click of her nails on the keyboard, or she is blowing out the fire under the silver tea urn and I can still taste the cinnamon toast she offers me.

The following pictures of my mother complete the series and are so dramatic that I feel that they are invented and I might have the power to cancel them as one cuts a film. I am engaged to be married and my mother has plunged into the task of equipping me with an elaborate trousseau and arranging for a huge garden wedding. She is beside me while I stand for fittings and we shop together in a flurry of linen and damask. Together we watch the wedding presents line up on long tables in the library; each numbered and recorded, they look as joyless as wares on a department store counter. I feel that my mother is trying to find joy in the midst of this unaccustomed activity and that she is not succeeding. The small currency of existence usually disappointed her. This was her strength and her weakness, her wisdom and her inadequacy. Her sensitive antennae are alerted. Always overprotective, is she worried about my marriage? Or is she responding to the ugly prewar events in Europe that the rest of us manage to ignore? I am for once unshaken by her ill-concealed sadness and go on my heedless way. I am focused elsewhere.

The wedding day begins with a biblical downpour which never stopped. "Happy the bride the sun shines on—" What happens to the one in the rain? But my élan is undisturbed. Inside the slightly dripping marquee I am like a female knight encased in shining white satin, splendidly confident of victory. As my husband and I are about to drive away, through the streaming window of the car I noticed my mother for the first time that day. She is framed in the doorway and the brilliance of her beauty puts the rest of the family surrounding her in obscurity. She is dressed in pearl gray, with a large picture hat under which her hair looks blond again and her face unlined. It is the ideal costume for her and she seems to be presenting it to me, along with the rest of the day's setting that she worked so hard to achieve.

A week later, in Paris, my husband and I received the

news of my mother's unexpected death. I have often thought that her end bears some relation to her delicate sentient nature. The galvanized activities of her last days — all worldly games — were the thin ice coverings of life, opaque to most humans, but to her always transparent. Finally, even my father's earthy loving hold on her failed to snatch her back from the dark depths she had feared.

The concert was over. It is surprising that one's sensation of almost superhuman greatness evaporates at the instant the music ceases. With the others from my box, I inched along in the crowd toward the street. We were all headed toward the Plaza Hotel. It was warm, there had been a light rain and the streets shown wetly like melted tar. I walked beside the tall Churchillian man who had sat behind me at the concert. But the bond I had felt with him was gone and we conversed in a stilted manner about trivialities. As we reached The Plaza, the old-fashioned buggies with their horses and top-hatted drivers came into view. Their spindly shapes in the misty night looked both forlorn and rakish. They were as inappropriate against the skyscraper backdrop as was Madame Touroff's chair in my childhood home.

The thought of my mother was with me, but I did not long for her as someone close who has gone. Rather her memory made me think, in a rueful fashion, of missed opportunities. We are amateur jugglers without the skill to keep all the balls in the air at once, which makes us exclaim: *If only — ! If only I had been — ! If only I had foreseen — ! If only I had seized — ! If only I had known my mother when — !* I wish I knew her now.

CHAPTER IV

WITH MY MARRIAGE, THE HOME OF MY CHILDhood disappeared, although physically it remained and my father continued to live there. When I visited him, I was someone else who could recall uneasily a past belonging to a person who was intimately associated with me. The bedrooms in the rear of the apartment were now uninhabited. My parents' large room, vacated by my father, had chintz hangings that were almost new. I remembered my mother's pleasure at their purchase, and they, too, were reminders of the frailty of small projects which at a moment's notice can be obliterated by the final denial of death. Her dressing table mirror, before which Miss Nelly used to crimp her long hair with a curling iron, returned no one's face. Its clear surface reflected an empty room. Next came my bedroom, intact but lifeless, and the room that used to be Mademoiselle's, pillaged in recent years, turned into a storage place. My brother's room at the end of the long dark narrow corridor was still crammed with old newspapers, magazines, pamphlets, and railroad schedules he had collected and could never bear to throw out. A group of English prints depicting hunting scenes and hunt breakfasts adorned the walls. They were certainly inappropriate to him and to our way of life, but they had been endowed by time and habit with a naturalness that required no explanation. Across the hallway was the door that led to the servants' quarters, another land with all the cruel underprivilege and dinginess of a story by Dickens. In my childhood, I was not often permitted entrance to the kitchen. It was a nether world region presided over by a series of witchlike monsters with rags wrapped around their perspiring foreheads, who tended the perpetual flame of a huge stove that, in my memory, never slept. The electricity burned at all times in the kitchen as its window was on a shaft. I remember the smoky yellow atmosphere, the color of the moment that precedes a thunderstorm. All the maids' cubicles faced on the shaft also. It remains a puzzle to me how my parents, apparently kind and considerate, could live so insouciantly in their section of the apartment while close by this Dickensian world worked and slept, separated only by the barriers of ordinary doors.

In later years I was aware of all these rooms at the back of the apartment, but I avoided them as much as possible. They reminded me of those remains of houses, destroyed by demolition crews, but still resisting the blitz with a rise of gaily painted wall here, some small item of human habitation there. In this way I viewed the relics of my childhood from the opposite sidewalk of married life.

My bedroom used to be a shelter from which I emerged to take stock of the myriad childhood worlds outside. Only during illness and at night would it enclose me. And my dreams were far-flung. My retreat was so familiar that I ceased to see it, and in later years, when my father used it as a cloakroom, I would ask myself: were those looped yellow taffeta curtains always there? that skirted dressing table? the imitation French toile upholstery? the heavy mahogany bed jutting out from the wall like a hull? No, nothing had been changed, but how shabby and meaningless it looked, no longer a home to return to, but a neglected extra room, lacking personality and style. After adding my coat to the pile on the bed, I would hurry away, as uncomfortable as though I had seen an old unflattering photograph of myself that, fortunately, no one else was able to recognize.

My earliest nursery in the other apartment down the avenue was more spacious and less frivolous. Pictures of Red Riding Hood, Peter Pumpkin Eater, and a strawberry-ice-cream-pink-painted desk and matching chair that had appeared with my first days at kindergarten were its only gestures toward childishness. The chair had been smashed, I remember, by a strange doctor sitting on it as he prepared a syringe. I still see his long legs upset ceilingward as the seat collapsed beneath his bulk — an ugly comic strip vision with the needle flying from the doctor's hand like a lethal insect. The windows of that nursery faced east and I often saw the rising sun over the Queensboro Bridge. A small door bolted and chained gave on to an outdoor fire escape. It had a forlorn institutional look.

Here, a bout of scarlet fever once lorded it over my other childhood diseases, an evil despot obliterating the memory of the small luxuries and indulgences of head colds and grippes. In those days, the contagion from scarlet fever was feared like the plague, or worse; the victim became a type of leper, his everyday associates fleeing, his surroundings contaminated. After the dread diagnosis, I remember that my brother was sent from the house to a hotel with our governess. My parents, I believe, remained behind, but I don't remember their company. I imagine that, like the Rostov family during the burning of Moscow, they clung to their beleaguered home from which all normal life had vanished. I was left to the care of Mrs. Taylor, a trained nurse, the leading lady of our childhood ills, who stood between us and our mother's uncontrollable fear of sickness. I know that she was there, but at this time even her reassuring presence was reduced to a shadow while the tyrannical illness imposed its laws. Everything I touched had to eventually be burned, and the doomed objects assumed new value and poignancy, like people parting on a railroad platform: — my dolls, the waxy-lidded twin infants, the loose-limbed flapper, her Pierrot-like pallor punctuated by a jet beauty spot. Only Jo-Jo, my favorite, a life-sized strapping baby boy with a complete, unbecoming, effete wardrobe had been smuggled out. He would survive the holocaust. My chief distraction was *The Secret Garden.* I had it read and reread to me, knowing that it would go too. It never occurred to me that it might be replaced. This particular book was my companion, unique; it filled my amorphous days and at night I dreamed of a dark, mysterious, enclosed garden, sealed by a little gate with a secret key. I still recall a lame boy, fragile and eager, hovering over the story that had become more real than my nursery with the shades lowered to protect my eyes from glare. The climax of the illness was the occurrence of a total eclipse of the sun. Then the shades were raised to show me this night-in-day. The murky eeriness of the noon-darkening sky where the sun was dwindling away to a small white lunar disc before totally dissolving over the rooftops and the skeletal towers of the Queensboro Bridge was no more weird than the tempo of my days and nights. It seemed an external outgrowth of my existence, a sickroom projection into the heavens. After the prescribed six weeks, a lady from the Board of Health came to inspect the premises, assuring herself of adequate destruction and examining the peeling skin on my hands to make sure that all was going according to schedule. Then, impersonal and firm as a warden, she departed and I was released, weak and dazed, to the outside world. And Mrs. Taylor was free to return home. But at the first cough, sneeze, or sign of chill, she would reappear on cue. Her entrance was indicated by the thermometer, like a conductor's baton. It had the power to make my mother turn pale, to produce that look of panic in her eyes, and to hold me in my bed until the bar of mercury descended to normal.

Mrs. Taylor was known to my brother and me, for some unknown reason, as "Meress." With her appearance, the atmosphere would lift. She was a small, slender young Irish American, but she had disproportionately broad hips and sturdy legs, which gave her body the shape of a pear. I see her in her starched white uniform, creased only across her ample buttocks in parallel lines that looked like the bars, without the notes, on a sheet of music. She had a perky triangular face, ending in a small determined pointed chin, green eyes, and dark bobbed hair with flapper spit curls on her cheeks. She would enter the nursery, singing songs from recently bygone times — mostly airs from World War I, such as "It's a Long Way to Tipperary" or "Hinky, Dinky, Parlez-Vous." My brother and I knew that she had been a nurse for the United States Army in France, where she had met her husband, George Taylor, a good-looking American soldier who had been severely gassed and was still suffering from the effects and unable to work. This was the reason for Mrs. Taylor's periodic appearance at our house. She also had a small son, named Buddy, in commemoration of his parents' wartime romance. When she was taking care of us, Buddy was boarded out with relatives. I never saw him, but I pictured him blond, blue-eyed, and delicate like his father, who stayed home all the time, incapacitated, coughing out his lungs, and dreaming of muddy trenches, olive-drab uniforms, barbed-wire fences, red poppies, and the cheerfulness of Mary Taylor, dancing along the lines of army cots like a restorative arrow of American sunshine.

There were moments when I felt guilty about this state of affairs and ashamed of my mother's cowardly retreat. But I vaguely sensed that it was connected, in some way, with the fading tragedy of the untimely death of her brother Richard, the perpetual mourning in the house on Sixty-second Street, the mystery of the smell of drugs in her sister Fanny's room, and her own unlabeled malaises. I had heard that on her wedding trip in London, she had experienced one of those hinted-at collapses. On the rare occasions it was mentioned, it was glossed over with references to the kindly distinguished doctors on Harley Street and the lovely peace and cleanliness of an English nursing home — quite as though doctors and nursing home were part of a London honeymoon and as much fun as shopping for English antiques and tea and crumpets at country inns.

So Mrs. Taylor became a leading lady. Early in her engagement with our family, an event took place that was barely understood by my brother and me. We were both down with measles and Meress was in attendance as always. She had made her usual entrance, singing "Mademoiselle from Armentières" in her cracked voice, with her abominable French accent. Although recently she had been looking a little plumper than usual, the outlines of her pear-shaped body were not markedly altered. But one noon, as we were sitting up in our beds, with our invalid lunch trays bridging our laps, Mrs. Taylor hurriedly left the nursery. We heard whispering and running footsteps outside the door, and then it was Tini, the French maid, who removed our trays, telling us that Mrs. Taylor had been suddenly called away. Somehow we managed to pass the prescribed time allotted to measles without her. When Meress made her next appearance, Buddy had entered her life, and ours, too, in that remote region where George Taylor also existed, sharing with us, without complaint, the cheerful helpfulness of Mary Taylor.

Meress made her final exit from our lives with equal suddenness. About five years after the birth of Buddy she was all at once taken sick at our house. I remember the shocking, unprecedented sound of her retching in the bathroom. Afterward, she was assisted from our quarters, leaning on Tini's stout dependable shoulder. She left wearing a parrot-green dress that accentuated the unusual pallor of her face. In spite of its vividness, the dress looked so much less cheerful than her white uniform with the familiar parallel creases across the rear.

Mrs. Taylor never appeared again. Later we were told that she had died of kidney disease. It seems ironic that Meress, a bulwark against our illnesses, had herself succumbed so quickly and so young. There is no dodging life's treacheries. With Mrs. Taylor's death, an irreplaceable leading lady was lost. For a while I wondered what had become of her ailing husband and small Buddy. Then I forgot all of it: the overseas romance, the rollicking war tunes sung in Mrs. Taylor's cracked voice, her dancing steps. It was all part of an act folded long ago that was played in the sunny confines of a nursery, to the hissing of a croup kettle in an atmosphere pungent with the fumes of benzoin.

Dr. Serge Dorfman played the leading man to Mary Taylor's leading lady, but he outlasted her by many years, and, only slightly altered, entered my adult life also. When I walk on upper Park Avenue, it still remains Dr. Dorfman's territory. He held sway there for over half a century and for many years I was one of his loyal subjects. Today the brass plate in front of his office reads, "Dr. Rufus Pearson," but even now, long after Dr. Dorfman's death, I am not convinced. The engraved nameplate has no more relation to the true composition of that place than the scrawled hieroglyphics on Dr. Dorfman's prescription pad had to the substance of the pills and potions he recommended.

My introduction to him when I was a small child is one of my earliest memories. I was emerging from ether after a tonsillectomy. It was a kind of original birth, an awakening from the mysteries of unconsciousness, since memory can throw no light on the biologically true one. As I struggled out of the mottled darkness, I felt a cool touch on my wrist and I heard a voice saying to a shadowy attendant, "When she can swallow, let her have some cold milk." It was a baptism ordered by a godlike being. I strained to see: slowly my nursery came into focus, and bending over me was a stranger in a white coat. His face was blurred, but I was transfixed by his eyes; sparkling and penetrating and reassuring, they communicated a message: you have come to safe harbor because I am here. "I am Doctor Dorfman," he said.

All through my life, when any member of my family fell ill, Dr. Dorfman would appear like an immaculate genie. I admired his irregular face, with a domed forehead, a hawk's nose, glowing skin, and a little goatee stuck to his chin like a tuft of sterile cotton — and always those ripe cherry eyes that hypnotized you into the belief that he could perform miracles. Any fever you might have was only a prop for the demonstration of a show he delighted in performing.

The office on Park Avenue was disorderly and unorthodox, but his patients had faith in its supernatural properties. Dr. Dorfman's secretary-nurse, Judy Brown, was in charge.

Equally disorderly and unorthodox, being technically neither nurse nor secretary, she qualified for the position through many years of fanatical devotion to Dr. Dorfman. She was invariably dressed in a dusty black sweater and skirt, and she slouched, sometimes with a lighted cigarette dangling from her mouth, from waiting room to office to examining room. Her ugliness was extravagant and she reminded me of the witch in "Hansel and Gretel."

For me, the heart of the office was a small windowless antechamber with a separate entrance. It contained a couch and an antiquated metabolism machine, part of which consisted of a discarded cookie tin. As you lay on the couch, your eyes rested on a large lithograph of the "Isle of the Dead," but you were confident, as you dutifully inhaled and exhaled, at Dr. Dorfman's behest, that his presence would be a barrier against that fatal journey, represented in the picture by a frail bark on a dark lake, heading toward an island spiked by black cypress. The antechamber had another interesting aspect. I had heard that Dr. Dorfman, always the champion of romance, loaned it to homeless lovers. He had a special feeling for lady patients with amatory problems. "She was a dear little thing," he would say of some Russian actress, "and there I found her fainted away on the floor, with a revolver in her hand. She had tried to shoot her lover." Sometimes, he would look at me, with a diagnostician's eye and a slight twinkle, saying, "You are a queer duck." And I wondered if, perhaps, that meant I was developing temperament, like the tempestuous ladies who were able to stir his imagination.

But he was no mere spectator; he had his own legend, which was intertwined with the Kuppermans' chronicle. Although the Dorfmans were comfortably bourgeois too, they had a predilection for the arts. Dr. Dorfman played the violin, his brother Albert, the ascetic, saintly, black-cloaked painter (once married to a cousin of my father's), had a partly American-Indian sculptress for his second wife. Dr. Dorfman's sister, Cecilia, was married to another relative of my father's, and from her well-upholstered vantage operated a salon for opera singers and actors. In my childhood I thought of her as an actress too, with large brooding dark eyes, a hawk's nose like Dr. Dorfman's, and hair in a dramatic swoop over her forehead in the style of Theda Bara. It was said that the great Caruso had once kissed the hem of her skirt — which conjured up a delicious scene composed of red velvet, gold-tasseled cushions, muted lamps, pearls, champagne, and the intoxicating aftertaste of grand opera.

The romantic story of Dr. Dorfman began many years before in Heidelberg, where he and his identical twin, Julian, had been sent to study medicine. There they met and wooed twin sisters. In my mind's eye I saw them (German "Gretchens" with ropes of flaxen hair), sitting with Serge and Julian (younger representations of themselves) in a field studded with wildflowers, or wandering arm in arm up the steep medieval streets of Heidelberg. Julian became a biologist in the Middle West, sent for Christina, and married her. Hedwig also came to the United States, but by that time Serge had caught a glimpse of Beatrice, my father's sister, at a bowling party. Although she was engaged to another man, he had been silently, irrevocably smitten; he explained to Hedwig that he would keep his vow to her, but that he loved another. So began an era of languors, sighs, and later, secret meetings that must have suited the romantic nature of Dr. Dorfman. The story was pieced together through the years, but it was difficult to place the beneficient Dr. Dorfman, my enigmatic, dumpy, sallow aunt, and the polite elderly German lady as three points of a triangle that endured, in varying lights and shadings, for almost half a century.

Like my father and Uncle Carl, Dr. Dorfman lived to be an octogenarian. Defying the laws of change and mortality, they presented a hedge against buried thoughts of death. They moved with determination in different but interlocking courses, sheltering me in their orbit like three homely earthbound guardian angels. They appeared cheerful. Unlike youth, old age cannot afford the luxury of melancholy. Toward the end of his life, Dr. Dorfman's hand did waver when he gave an injection and he was accompanied on his rounds by the faithful Judy Brown. But these seemed minor changes, and I agreed with my father, who each morning read the obituary page in the newspaper with a small gleam of triumph in his eyes. Decidedly, those who died deserved it. Somehow they had lacked the know-how to live on — the odd thing was that my father looked on Uncle Carl and Dr. Dorfman as old. Uncle Carl felt the same about my father and Dr. Dorfman. And Dr. Dorfman, on his professional calls on either of the other two, would inquire solicitously about the health of the "old man." It is said that a soldier in combat believes that the bullets will find the other one, but leave him standing. Yet within three years, my father, Uncle Carl, and Dr. Dorfman were gone —

I think of that old nursery as somber, probably because I seem to have spent so much time being ill there. And the move uptown to the yellow-curtained bedroom appears in retrospect, like a step from darkness to light, from sickness to health, from helplessness to cheerful activity. I was eight years old at the time, and group life, trying to learn from the observation of others, had set in. Relatives, school, and the little band of children I met each afternoon in Central Park formed my education.

Cousin Carmen (the same who had organized that disastrous theatrical venture for my grandfather in the Adirondacks) and her daughter Agnes were constantly around from the beginning. Carmen might have been classified as a somewhat "poor relation," but she was far from wearing the traditional, humble, apologetic mien of that breed. On the contrary, through my childhood, I had the feeling that she was the benefactor, the aggressor, the one who "knew how," while my mother and I followed where she gaily led us. Cousin Carmen and her sisters were also "Frank girls," her father having been my grandfather's first cousin. On the surface, one might have described them as the wrong side of the family, as Arabella, Carmen, Blanchette, and their widowed mother were as homely as Fanny, Rose, Sarah, Emily, and Hannah Frank had been beautiful. They might have played the ugly sisters to the composite Cinderella loveliness of the Isaac Frank women. But they thrived, while my mother's family was doomed to illness, early death, and eventual impoverishment. Carmen was of a parallel age to my mother, and my mother appeared to take heart from their kinship, while dutifulness to her own sisters must have been a painful burden assumed only because of a scrupulous conscience.

In the Leopold Frank family, Arabella was the oldest. I saw her rarely as she was childless. Ugly as a gargoyle, she and her husband owned an art gallery and lived in a downtown brownstone with community gardens in the back. Occasionally Agnes and I were permitted to play in the orderly long green strip. Blanchette, "the baby," was considered the family beauty. Everything is comparative, but it is nonetheless difficult to see how she had earned this title as she was almost as homely as her sisters, sharing their beak noses and thick lips. But she was blond and gregarious and had made a rich marriage. Arabella and Carmen, while conscious that they moved in the superior world of the arts, did not look down on Blanchette's worldly success. Selma, their ancient mother, survived to be almost one hundred. I remember her as a shriveled version of her daughters, living, apparently forever, in an apartment hotel. Sometimes I accompanied Agnes on a ceremonial call and I marveled at old Selma's shrunken head, as brown and wrinkled as a walnut shell.

But Cousin Carmen's family was peripheral to me, while she was central and omnipresent, my mother's afterimage, and a total contrast: certain, while my mother hesitated, thick-skinned, where my mother lacked an epidermis, extravagantly ugly, while my mother was gently beautiful. Cousin Carmen was a self-creation. At all times she wore a mask, gay and stylized, a theater emblem. My mother's nature was precariously open, a prey to her surroundings, and in spite of her naturally superior endowments, I believe she was impressed by Carmen's impudent verve and daring.

In many ways Cousin Carmen was a forerunner Women's Liberation type. In her youth she had been an apprentice to the illustrious social worker, Agnes Stein, and through her had been introduced to a "neighborhood" theater in Henry Street. That enterprise had grown into the Community Playhouse School of the Theatre and, in my day, Carmen was its director. Agnes Stein had become a distant sun in Carmen's sky, but her influence never entirely disappeared. Carmen had named her daughter after her. I met Miss Stein once when she was old and fat and it was hard for me to understand how this scrubbed unadorned woman had any connection with Cousin Carmen's grease paint world of the stage. Looking back, I suspect that Carmen might have been sexually androgynous. I realized that Agnes Roth had been the central love of her life and that her brief marriage (from which Agnes was the result) had been a mere bagatelle. It was a standard anecdote in our family that Cousin Carmen had confided to my mother that on her nuptial bed she had been obliged to "laugh at the whole performance" and that "poor Maximilian had taken offense." It was obvious that the unfortunate groom lacked a sense of humor!

Without talent herself, Carmen had thrown herself into the world of the theater. A galaxy of stars had been hatched from her school, and I early grew to know that "Gregory," "Martha," "Kit," and "Charley" were the famous actors we saw as finished products behind the footlights. Cousin Carmen would make a familiar sniffing sound through her long nose and her prominent brown eyes would kindle as she said, in her acquired British accent with careful diction, "Martha" (or "Charley" or "Kit," as the case might be) "is a stunning person!" — a standard phrase with her. She was the archetypal lion hunter, name-dropper, culture vulture, a latter-day Madame Verdurin. Her small rotund person with large pendulous breasts and disproportionately dainty feet reigned over the little circle in her apartment, modest in rent, but rich in "art." It was a contrast to our life-style, and like my mother, I always felt I had much to learn from Cousin Carmen and her surroundings.

My mother had a habit of saying wistfully that Carmen had a genuine flair for interior decoration. Her apartment was small, a stereotype on a side street in the East Seventies. But it was filled with "art objects" never seen in the homes of other friends and relatives. A terra cotta head of a woman dominated the living room. She looked emaciated and sad, like a Modigliani creation, a reminder to the rest of the cheerfully decorated room that art can be melancholy even while it transcends. Our rooms at home were somber, and no work of art pierced the gloomy uniformity of puce velvet and steely gray brocade. Our dining room was always electrically lit (since it faced the shaft); our table was invariably covered by a white cloth and set with conventional crystal and English china. Cousin Carmen's dining room was as obscure as a robber's den, perceived through the wavering glow of candles. Place mats were made of straw, the goblets ruby red, and the dishes of thick Mexican pottery illustrated with "amusing" primitive designs.

When one entered Agnes' room, one was inside a Swiss chalet. The matching furniture was painted bright blue. Peasant style, a Madonna and Child graced the doors of the wardrobe; red hearts and multicolored garlands clambered over the other pieces. I accepted this décor as I did the members of Cousin Carmen's clan, as part of her "flair." I sometimes encountered Sandy White, a drama coach at the school. He had a naked hairless head, was as round and boneless as Humpty Dumpty, and spoke in a eunuch's high falsetto. Irene Cohen possessed legendary wealth and largely subsidized the school. Also an early follower of Agnes Stein, she was a spinster dressed in flowing black garments, her straight black hair looped from a center part like curtains on either side of her face and gathered into a bun at the nape of her neck. She was as emaciated as the terra cotta statue, but she lacked its transcendental aura, for she appeared to be perpetually grieving. Then there were assorted artists, young dancers with overdeveloped calves and behinds like jutting shelves, an aging actress with a voice that resonated like church bells in a valley, and youthful would-be actors and actresses, enthusiastically applying the Stanislavsky method to each everyday act. A simple command, like "pass the butter," was loaded with meaning and accompanied by gestures that studiously symbolized the entire past of the speaker, his accumulated aspirations and fears, his background, his love life on up to what he had eaten that morning for breakfast.

Agnes and I mutely watched these gatherings in her home, part of them, yet outsiders, while Cousin Carmen was central, punctuating the lively chatter with her usual exclamations: "Stunning!" "Thrilling!" "A real person!" "Exciting breakthrough!" "Handles herself well!" — or not, as the case might be. "An artist to his very fingertips!"

Carmen's enthusiasm extended to engulf Agnes also. Perhaps due to the unreality of her marriage and the insignificance of the long-divorced but unlamented Maximilian, Carmen regarded Agnes, buxom and bovine, as her private miracle. Her daughter's pug nose, rosy cheeks, blue eyes, and fair hair constituted an artistic masterpiece. And the fact that Agnes did not seem to possess any particular talent did not worry Cousin Carmen. She was confident that by constant exposure, Agnes would develop artistic ability by osmosis. She and I would allow ourselves to be dragged backstage after a performance by some Community Playhouse School of the Theatre graduate or teacher. I suffered at those times from extreme awkwardness and embarrassment. And when I was old enough to say no, Agnes was obliged to go without me. As soon as the curtain was lowered and before the applause had faded away, Cousin Carmen, shoving Agnes and me in front of her, would head in the opposite direction from the rest of the audience. By a little side door, we arrived behind the scenes, a fascinating world of levers, ropes, ladders, platforms, and screens manned by sweating technicians. We never lingered here, but proceeded down spirals of iron stairs through a maze of subterranean corridors, gallantly led by Cousin Carmen, into the very sanctuary of the star's dressing room. There, instead of Juliet or Cleopatra, we found an older woman removing her false eyelashes. She would appear exhausted but elated. Cousin Carmen hurled herself into her arms crying, "Darling, you were heavenly, unsurpassed, inspired — a thrilling performance — and the girls want to congratulate you too!" Agnes and I were pushed forward, helpless and tongue-tied, and the great actress would lower her weary painted eyes to ours. We were enveloped by the smell of grease paint, cold cream, and perfume. I had no words of felicitation, but I wanted to apologize for our intruding presence and for the dispersion of the exciting illusion we had witnessed out front.

Cousin Carmen and my mother formed two pillars on the steps of my learning and growing up. I know now that Cousin Carmen's influence was a by-product of her own ego and personal ambition. Agnes and I were caught up in her élan, like courtiers in a sultan's train. I have come to realize that her audacity and energy were probably the other side of her insecurity as a woman — the results of her grotesque ugliness and worldly deficits that she was able to exchange with so much gaiety and dexterity for the shining counterfeit gold coin of her "world of the arts." My mother, on the other hand, instructed me conscientiously, selflessly, with anxiety and much love. I resisted her teachings, but I have come to appreciate them years later.

I remember that we were on a channel boat between England and France when my mother attempted to tell me the facts of life. It was my first summer in Europe and I must have been about seven years old. Why she chose that time and that place, what led up to her talk, I can no longer remember. But I recalled the sickish rise and fall of the steely white-flecked water and the prickly sensation of the rope attached to a life preserver that I was playing with. I could still feel the wet air and taste the salt on my lips. My mother was patiently explaining the process of reproduction with the help of examples from plant and insect life. Every now and then she would pause and ask, "Is that clear? Do you understand?" I invariably assented, although my mind was a jumble of protests. It was all impossible! Never before had my mother seemed so alien. I tried not to listen, yet at the same time her words drew me. But I could not look at her face. I kept my eyes steadily ahead, where the shore of France, a hazy line, was appearing, and when I could distinguish the first dotting of houses, I could bear it no longer. I turned around and announced, "I'm going to the other side of the boat and look at land from there."

"I haven't finished yet," my mother said, but she sounded relieved and she did not try to restrain me.

"I know all that stuff anyway," I lied, before galloping around the corner of the deck.

My mother did not resume the lesson and it was buried in my mind with other odds and ends until one afternoon in the Engadine. It might have been later that same summer, or perhaps, the summer after. We were living in a big hotel with a view of snowcapped mountains and dark pine forests, a half-hour's walk from the village. Our balcony, where we breakfasted on melting croissants and black cherry jam, overlooked a valley that sounded all day long with church chimes and cowbells. But the hotel interior and its guests were more interesting to me at this time than all the lavish alpine scenery. The lobby, particularly at teatime, had a special fascination. It was an enormous wood-paneled room, hung with antlers and cuckoo clocks. Waiters threaded their way through a maze of small tables arranged around a clearing in the center of the floor. Every afternoon the hotel guests and other summer tourists from the town gathered here for dancing. Always present were three men, all polished dancers. I had asked my mother who they were and she had told me they were called gigolos and were paid to dance with the guests. One had pomaded yellow hair, one black hair, and one a shining smooth crown. Yet they looked curiously alike, in suits with padded shoulders and nipped waists. Sometimes in the morning they sunned themselves by the tennis court in silk sport shirts with monogrammed pockets. With the strictness of childhood, I disapproved of their life and their appearance, yet I watched them whenever I could. They were as interesting as figures in *Grimm's Fairy-Tales*, and like these, their number was three. I remember that there were always three princes, three brothers changed into frogs, or three wicked sisters.

One afternoon, my brother, another girl, and I, accompanied by Mademoiselle, were returning to the hotel from a walk in the village. We knew every inch of the way because Mademoiselle was an inveterate hiker and fervently believed in "plenty of fresh mountain air." As we marched up the street, the feeling of each uneven cobblestone was familiar to the soles of our feet.

Suddenly my brother stopped, pointing. "Look what those two dogs are doing," he said.

We all stared until Mademoiselle pushed us roughly ahead. "What dirtiness!" she exclaimed. "Move along, quick!"

"Why they're only —" my friend began.

But Mademoiselle interrupted her, "Don't say it! Walk!"

As usual, I smarted at Mademoiselle's orders, but now, unaccountably, I felt a sick longing to be far away. My mother's talk on the boat returned to me. With a tingling of disgust I wondered: Was this what she had been trying to tell me? Were people like this too — like animals?

When we reached the hotel, the tea hour was in full swing. Of course, The Blond, The Dark, and The Bald were there, engaged in polite conversation with three no-longer-young ladies dressed in pastel cashmere and pearls. To me they were a welcome sight. Ignoring the urging of my companions, I sat down on a chair against a wooden pillar and looked around with satisfaction, clinging to my ignorance for an antidote. No, people were not like the dogs in the village street. They were different. People were like this.

When I was fourteen, I visited my relatives in California. I no longer had as much time for the imaginative reflection about the grown-up world that had occupied me when I was younger. Life had become more prosaic and I was, at once, more unthinking and more fearless. My cousin was already interested in the snaring of the male species. I followed her lead, not yet understanding, but admiring and imitating. I remember the morning we went alone to a department store in San Francisco and bought ourselves Empress Eugenie hats, in vogue at that time. Marian's was a brown derby with a limp yellow bird falling precariously over one eye, and mine, a navy tricorn with a white dove (complete with shiny black beak and eyes) nestled in its brim. We felt exhilarated, and on the way home we stopped at the Five and Ten and Marian bought me a Tangee lipstick — my first. I remember that it was the color of orange marmalade and tasted like perfumed disinfectant. We were women of the world and we hoped that all the men in the street were staring at us with longing. But when we reached home, our parents, half laughing, half appalled, removed our new hats and the Tangee was scrubbed from my lips until they burned. I wasn't permitted to use it again, but I kept it for a long time. It looked like a silver cartridge lying at the bottom of my jewel box.

The following winter, in preparation for my becoming a woman, my mother had me take lessons in interpretative dancing, at Cousin Carmen's suggestion. There were five girls in the class, all of us on the wavering borderline between childhood and adolescence — and these lessons were supposed to give us enough poise to take the next step gracefully. So far we were just muscle sore. The stiffness would be just receding when Monday afternoon rolled around again. At the end of the hour's exertion in Jane Gordon's studio, we stood with weak knees and tired backs in our severe, professional-looking black leotards, waiting for Kurt Widner (composer and Jane Gordon's accompanist) to play the dismissal chord on the piano. "Hold your heads proudly," Jane Gordon would order, "always look like the Winged Victory!" Then, with trembling legs, we ran to the dressing room to change our clothes and hurry through the darkening winter-damp streets, forgetting the Winged Victory in our longing for the indulgence of a hot bath.

Yet I always looked forward to Monday with a lift of spirit. I couldn't dance; the stretching and contorting on the studio floor belonged more to the gymnasium than to the stage. But Jane Gordon belonged to the stage — more than that, she was dedicated. I felt it although I couldn't define it. I admired it from my different world and humbly realized that she would not be giving us dancing lessons had it not been for Cousin Carmen's "contacts" through her theater school and if Jane Gordon had not needed the money. Artists were always poor; I had just read *Trilby*.

One February afternoon, arriving early, I dawdled up the stairs of the shabby house where Jane Gordon lived and worked, trying to remember how I would feel when I came down an hour later, hugging the banister for support. The house always smelled of the aftermath of cooking, combined with the odd musty odor of old metallic costumes and grease paint. And dust was everywhere—it coated the tall wooden doors and ran along the dark corridors. At the top of the stairs I overtook one of my classmates. I remember that her name was Flavia, that she was thin and pallid, could lose herself in the reading of *Idylls of the King*, was subject to fainting fits and colds, and had to wear white socks to dance.

Jane Gordon's bedroom was on our left and we noticed to-day that her door was blown ajar. We peeped through the opening. She lay on her back in the center of the big bed, her long black hair spread in a circle on the pillow like the rays of a mysterious dark sun. Her eyes were closed and her face looked shut, too, as if it held a secret. Kurt Widner sat on the edge of the bed, his fat pinkish chest and belly bulging out of his open shirt, his suspenders hanging slack from his unbuttoned trousers. He was bending over labori-ously to tie his shoelaces. One shoe lay on the floor next to the bed.

Flavia and I looked at each other guiltily and then hurried in silence to the dressing room. We sat on the broken-down brown corduroy couch and stared through the high windows that opened on nothing—the blank wall opposite. Then we both began at once, "How can she?" "That old man!" "He's so fat!" "Isn't it awful!" I had heard the rumor that Jane Gordon and Kurt Widner were lovers but I had staunchly refused to believe it. Now disgust mingled with the thrilling anticipation of breaking the news to the others.

Later, as we were all scrambling into our dancing costumes, a feeling of lonely disloyalty came over me. To what? Why? I didn't try to analyze it.

We were sitting, shivering slightly on the cold floor, when Jane Gordon and Kurt Widner appeared. Today, instead of the plain leotard, she wore a floating garment with red polka dots and her hair was tied back from her face in a scarlet ribbon. How often I had studied her face! And I always found something new: sometimes it belonged to a queen from ancient Egypt, sometimes the prominent cheekbones and gaunt cheeks became a stark theatrical mask. Today, polka dots, white face, black hair sleeked back from the high rounded forehead and full dark red lips made me think of a tragic clown.

We all watched her in silence as she moved across the floor to shut a window. Widner sat at the piano, idly playing chords. His pink jowls shook as his hands hit the keyboard. I looked away.

Jane Gordon joined us on the floor. "Ready for the first exercise," she said. "Everyone is very quiet this afternoon."

Dutifully we began. "One — and — stretch — and — bend — and —" she counted.

Whenever I could I stared at her, thinking about what I had just seen, wondering what she was thinking. Now with her draperies spread around her, her abstracted expression faraway, she reminded me of a beautiful convalescent.

At last she rose. "Stop the music, Kurt. There's no spirit in them today." Then turning around to us, she asked, "Shall I dance for *you* instead?"

We could barely assent. Such a gift had not been offered us before. We drew back to clear the floor and Kurt Widner began to play a Chopin polonaise. I can still recapture the sweet rousing strains.

At first I noticed many unrelated things: through the studio window I discovered a few stubborn patches of snow in Central Park, in Jane Gordon's movements I recognized the transformation of some of the angular exercises we had been doing. I studied her feet, square and strong, thick as a panther's paws, the soles already black from the grimy boards. Then all of a sudden, the music and the dance took possession of me, throbbing and forceful; they were one, and I was one with them — pausing and advancing, again and again — free of the earth, yet of the earth. In that moment I thought I understood the relationship of Jane Gordon and Kurt Widner. I no longer repudiated it. I exulted in it. It was part of something I had never understood until now — something that I would know some day, be part of too. All the small divinations of my childhood culminated in one divination. I comprehended deeply.

During the winter season Cousin Carmen made many contributions to my education: Jane Gordon, outstandingly, but also, an acting group taught by the lady with the resonant voice. I still feel today the correct vibration in my nasal passages when I recite again: *She left the web, she left the loom, she made three paces thro' the room, she saw the water lily bloom, she was the lady of Shalott.* For weeks during the summer Cousin Carmen and Agnes accepted our hospitality, living in the country houses my parents rented for the time before our trips to Europe. But even then Cousin Carmen made me feel that she was doing us a favor, my mother benefiting from her lively company. I knew she considered me puny and high-strung, and in some way, I was supposed to gain from Agnes' poundage and placid temperament.

One June we leased a house from a distant cousin of my mother's, a widower, rich and a notorious miser. It rises large in my memory as it did on a grassy hill in Connecticut. I do not understand its importance, but I have learned to respect those stubborn memory pictures and trust the validity of their involuntary brightness more than the deliberate recall of important events whose abstract meanings are fading fast. I have come across "Windy Corners" in the dark places of the past, and it is a find, like the dusty lamps and old bedsteads Agnes and I used to discover in the attics of the houses my parents rented.

It was a neoclassical structure of gigantic proportions, with hollow-looking pillars and a flat roof, a copy of the Petit Trianon. Our cousin, true to type, had newly painted the front facing the road an improbable pink — perhaps a bad imitation of marble. But the rear, for reasons of economy, had been left a dull elephant gray, peeling in many places and giving the huge sides of the house a look of an ancient molting animal. But the grass was always greenest in June and the day after the release from city and school, deliciously extended, an eternity of leafiness and blue sky. There were also the charms of books discovered in the libraries of rented houses; shabby, second-class fare, I read them all, and they filled an occasional rainy day with the voluptuous Peeping Tom pleasure of spying on the tastes of strangers.

On one of the spacious lawns surrounding the house we set up a croquet set and my mother, Cousin Carmen, Agnes, and I would play foursomes. The trim sound of wooden mallet against wooden ball is distinct to this day. And I remember the solemn ritual of choosing colors. My mother, Agnes, and I played seriously, but Cousin Carmen was given to chattering throughout, taking her bad shots lightly, and forgetting when it was her turn. I believe my mother's interest in simple games like croquet and solitaire was an antidote to her chronic worrying: a pretend set of problems, deliberately set up and neatly solved distracted her, and she could throw herself into them with a child's absorption. At these times Cousin Carmen was the odd adult and we united to criticize her interruptions and lack of concentration. As soon as the game was over, my mother returned to her preoccupations, large and small. That particular summer she reproached herself for the inadequacy of the house, its useless size, ugly pretentiousness, and drafty rooms. But Agnes and I found it fascinating, like an eccentric relative. One afternoon a thunderstorm overtook us at our game of croquet. The sky darkened dramatically, as, pelted by rain and wind, we ran for shelter. Inside the echoing living room we attempted to secure the windows, but they were warped and kept blowing open against our efforts. The sparse featherweight straw furniture skidded around in the gale like autumn leaves.

"What are we doing in this mausoleum?" my mother dolefully asked. "I never should have taken it."

Here Cousin Carmen took over. "I like it," she stated firmly and began piling the wicker chairs one upon the other for weight. I see her long earrings dangling, her protruding brown eyes sparkling, her small roly-poly body, clothed in Hannah batik print, darting with agility over the slippery bare floor. And soon the room was cleared as for a ball and all four of us were laughing hilariously as the wind kept on blowing open one window after another. The afternoon had turned into one of those "demonstrations" I had seen at Cousin Carmen's school, enjoyed so much more by the participants than by the audience. And I have retained a clear memory of this small sample of Cousin Carmen's spirit, returned to me through the years on the back of the sultry wind, to the sound of thunder and the dry skittering of straw furniture in the drafty living room of a summer house that still stands in my memory.

After my mother's death and with Agnes and me growing up, I saw Cousin Carmen more and more infrequently. I know that Agnes married a lawyer and lives a domestic life in the suburbs. This must have disappointed Cousin Carmen, but I suspect that Agnes was relieved to be shed of that world of "art" and "artists," always alien to her, and of her mother's attempts at the fanciful re-creation of her only child's buxom stolid person. And perhaps one of Agnes' four daughters might be molded into a "stunning person" indigenous to the theater world of Cousin Carmen.

My last view of Cousin Carmen, not long ago, took place

in a London hotel. My husband and I ran into her in the lobby one evening. Now retired from her post as director of the Theatre School, she had become a very old lady. But she was still surrounded by a group of young actors of undetermined sex, her British accent, still vied with theirs, her diction was as careful as ever, and she still sniffed vehemently through her long nose. However, her face had altered, the gay theater mask had slipped awry, revealing the desolate reality of lonely old age. The clever brown eyes looked frightened now — wrinkled and thinner, she reminded me of the ancient Selma. She was introducing my husband and me to her entourage, jauntily trying to push the mask back into place. From the past I seemed to hear the names of "Gregory," "Martha," "Kit," and "Charley." "They are telling me," Cousin Carmen was saying, "about plans for a thrilling new performance."

From the nursery I was sent to the Thomas Jefferson School. Looking back, it appears unsurpassed in size and gloom. There must be some law directing our fortunes because when luck is with us, all happy things accrue to us and we have the illusion that we are coordinating easily with the universe, moving near the sky, high above the crowd like tightrope walkers defying the possibility of a fall. But at other times combinations are wrong, and like bicyclists off balance, we lurch helplessly from side to side, losing confidence — a bit more at each bend of the road. At the Thomas Jefferson School I felt that luck had deserted me. As soon as the door closed behind me, I was in prison. It was an imposing dingy building, so far uptown, in such an unfamiliar neighborhood, that I had the impression that I was in a foreign city. It was called a "semi-public school" and its selection still puzzles me. It seems a rude departure from my cosseted upbringing. My parents, or rather my mother (my father rarely involved himself with the problems of our education), must have chosen it on the theoretical belief that an early indoctrination into the workings of democracy was essential to learning, an ethical thought, not inconsistent with my mother's nature, but at complete variance with the rest of my life. Also included among my mother's anxieties was the fear of social rebuff because of our being Jewish. The student body at the Thomas Jefferson School was a "cross section," economic, social, racial. We would meet each morning and in the afternoon disperse to the separate geographies of our homes, each section of the city being a small independent nation. My family's trusted chauffeur, Kevin, was delegated liaison officer between Park Avenue and upper Broadway. Never did he look so reassuring and lovable as when the moment came to part at the solemn entrance. I would have liked to cling to his solid body, to burrow under the fur lap robe in order to avoid the fatal step inside. But Kevin's broad face and his kind blue eyes behind his shining glasses were impervious to my desperation, propelling me forward without any realization of my daily act of heroism. The school was an old-fashioned academic institution whose cavernous front hall was blocked by the torso of the Venus of Milo. Her one-armed white marble presence was a chilly good morning and the chalky musty air in the dark corridors stuck in my throat and made me fear I would gag. But it was through another that my apprehensions were confirmed. We would assemble in our vast classroom at desks that were clamped to the floor, as were our chairs. The first-grade teacher, her blond pompadour like an unripe pumpkin outlined against the blackboard, presided over us on a dais. We would be called upon to recite the lesson when we raised our hands and our hands must be raised also if we wished, for any reason, to leave our riveted seats. Not long after the opening of school, I noticed a black-haired boy with vivid red cheeks. He was situated on an aisle beneath one of the large institutional windows. His hand had been raised for some time, but Miss Robbins chose to ignore it, as she inscribed meaningless numbers on the blackboard and then obliterated them with an expert motion of the eraser that sent the white dust flying into our faces. The boy's raised hand was becoming a frantic flapping. Then I saw him rise to his feet with slow-motion dignity, as with the same slow motion he proceeded to vomit over the floor. I can still hear the shocking splatter as it hit the bare boards, see the horrifying cascade and the apologetic panic in the boy's round brown eyes, before Miss Robbins, aroused at last, hurried him from the classroom. It was my first awareness of rigid conformity and the risk of its being shattered, all in a moment, by the sudden violence of an uncontrollable event. Any one of us might have been the victim. When would my turn come? I lasted at the Thomas Jefferson School (with many falterings and sham illnesses) until the fourth grade, when in the middle of a term, like a refugee, I migrated to the "progressive" liberty of the Weston School.

My initial glimpse was an oasis. In its infancy, at that time, the school occupied two ramshackle brownstones on the West side at Seventy-second Street. The move to the new ten-story red brick building across the park was still several years off. I remember the location of each room and the covered boardwalk connecting the two houses in the rear. I was shown first into the history "laboratory," where the teacher was informally surrounded by her circle of experts. A "conference" on China was under way and enthusiasm ran high. In retrospect, I see Mrs. Gignoux as a shepherd-guru to her flock. But she looked like a female King Lear, with wild locks and distracted eyes, and her patient voice was overpowered by her exuberant pupils. I watched and listened avidly. This noisy spontaneous helter-skelter spectacle was a far cry from the classroom I had left. For the first time the desire to participate replaced the prayer to be overlooked. The wobbly bicycle had been abandoned at the dark threshold of the Thomas Jefferson School.

If the history laboratory was an oasis, the English laboratory was my haven. Here children were stretched out reading on shabby cretonne cushions in the embrasures of the bow windows. It was not a schoolroom but a welcoming living room where the imagination was expertly nurtured, like the green plants in front of the unused Victorian fireplace. I was seated at a table and asked whether I wanted to write "The Life of a Penny." In spite of the newness of my surroundings, I felt almost confident and experienced, a lift of heart at the promise of my own untried possibilities. Next to me, a girl with a snub nose, freckles, and curly hair was absorbed in her creation. She looked up when I sat down and said, "Shall I read you my story?" The last line is with me still, *And then by the light of the moon, they slowly revolved around the Sphinx.* To this day, no poem has appeared more beautiful to me.

In the new building, the second floor was the heart of the school. On the right-hand side of the corridor, two double black portals led to the balcony of the assembly room, a perfect reproduction of a real theater, with a full-size stage, lights, and scarlet curtain. Years later I heard that it was considered obsolete and money was needed for improvement. But when it was new, it was a modern marvel — in lacquer black, red, and white. At the Weston School, I loved the formality of the weekly assemblies, when we would march into the auditorium, single file, shortest first, tallest last — ritual without reason. The martial piano music that accompanied our orderly entrance filled us with pride and solemnity. It was a temporary relief from freedom, a tiny taste of the forbidden fruit of conformity. My moments of greatest triumph took place here, when I dropped my everyday self and appeared on the stage, beneath the professional floodlights, costumed, painted, representing a Greek amazon, Betsy Ross, or a medieval princess before a hushed, shadowy audience. At the Weston School, everyone was a potential star.

The second floor used to combine modernity and newness

with an ancient veiled message from the Far East. Our principal, Martha Elmhurst (the originator of the Weston Plan), a spinster from Kansas, with a stray spark surprisingly contained in her elephantine person, had returned from a visit to Japan, China, and India, in the reversed role of missionary from East to West. A large Buddha had made its appearance at the end of the hall. It glowed under artistic lights and seemed to be surveying enigmatically the comings and goings of the Weston boys and girls, like an old tree rooted in the midst of the twitterings and flutterings of birds. Miss Elmhurst had even consecrated a small room adjacent to the assembly for the purpose of meditation. It was bare and blue — blue floor, ceiling, walls — and we were supposed to drop into its tiny limitlessness for renewal and inward quiet. But the meditation room proved to be one of Miss Elmhurst's follies, her missionary spirit having gotten the better of her common sense. The sanctuary was maltreated by her obtuse Western students as a place for the telling of dirty jokes and gossip! We would rustle in, in our starched green smocks, looking serious and holy, but suppressed giggles could be heard issuing from behind the closed door. And the meditation room disappeared as suddenly as it had appeared, its hazy blue horizon melting away into the poster-paint colors of the rest of the school.

In my last years at the Weston School, the literature room, also on the second floor, presided over by Mr. Gopal Chatterji, another import from India, and the science laboratory, under the supervision of Dr. Boris Borodine, were two exotic lands holding for me, at different times, the promise and uncertain joys of love.

As from a great distance, I glimpse Mr. Chatterji, sitting tailorwise on the floor in a semilotus position. In all likelihood, he really sat conventionally on a chair, behind a table, facing us, a group of adolescent girls — his pupils. But in the camera lens of the years, memory makes fixed pictures, not necessarily true, but more enduring than facts, many of which elude me now, as unsubstantial and dispersible as dandelion puffs. Mr. Chatterji remains a small, indelible image in my recollection: his great glowing black eyes looking out of his beautiful and aristocratic chocolate-brown face held all the secrets of the universe, and the answers, in his hypnotic philosophy, changed back into questions. He was a Brahmin, high caste — for me, synonymous with Prince — and he condescended to us middle-class Western schoolgirls. But he never stooped to talk down. Like the enigmatic Buddha in the alcove at the end of the hall, his eyes seemed to be saying: make of me what you can — I am a mystery and the world is a riddle, too — accept it. Actually, he had been engaged to teach us Shakespeare and Milton. He had an ugly, resentful attitude toward Shakespeare, saying, "Ladies, let us see what the old boy has to say today." And then in a mocking beautiful voice, with a cultivated British accent, he would read out loud, "The thane of Cawdor . . . ," making it sound like a parody. For *Paradise Lost,* on the other hand, he had admiration and respect, and the lines would roll over us like thunder from another planet. Fortunately for me, Shakespeare, in time, was able to free himself from the toils of the sarcastic Indian prince, but to this day, the lines of *Paradise Lost* retain some connection with Mr. Chatterji's compelling eyes, his sensuous curving mouth and aristocratic small-boned person, the Christian Lucifer forever blending with the image of the Hindu mystic, sitting immaterially but permanently in my memory, very straight, in the semilotus position.

Sometimes he would impatiently throw aside the book he was reading and fix his eyes on one or another of us. When my turn came, I felt myself immobilized in delicious paralysis. His words at those times were not abstractions but physical experiences, somber caresses. "I will tear away now the Veil of Maya that separates me from the truth. All the creatures of the earth will pass before me and I will say, 'There go I, there go I, there go I . . .'" I understood his message only dimly; nonetheless, it had a familiar ring. Deep down, it met the incantation of my childhood: *Who am I? I am nothing . . . I might have been a rock, a toad, a blade of grass . . .* I experienced for the stranger, Mr. Chatterji, an instant of piercing intimacy. When he removed his eyes, I awoke suddenly and wanted to beg him not to go away. But he would retrieve the crumpled book, saying, "Well, ladies, class is out for today."

Walking home down Park Avenue, with my special friend of the moment, I tried to carry out Mr. Chatterji's teachings. At a certain block we always met a beggar woman, a cripple, selling pencils. The upper part of her body was strong and stout and she had a ruddy peasant face, but she lacked legs and propelled herself on a board with roller-skate wheels. Remembering the words "There go I," I attempted to look her directly in the face, laying aside horror and pity. But failing utterly, I concentrated on the tin cup she held out and, hurriedly buying a pencil, listened to the jangle of my coin as it hit bottom. Further on, outside a grocery shop, two tiger cats surveyed us with clear yellow eyes. Now, perhaps, I might succeed in piercing the Veil of Maya! I paused, four eyes met mine unblinkingly — but my friend Susan was tugging at my elbow. "Quick, let's cross the street! You know that I'm deadly allergic to cats!" By the time we reached the other side of Park Avenue, Mr. Chatterji had been temporarily abandoned and Susan and I were busily inventing excuses to telephone a certain boy of our acquaintance, with whom we were both currently in love. Nevertheless, for me, a nagging sense of failure persisted.

The science laboratory was located near the stairs that led from the third-floor cafeteria. Outside the door the stale smell of stew and coffee wafted down. But inside, the special odors of the science room took over: a mixture of sulphur, alcohol from the Bunsen burners, and formaldehyde in which the frogs to be dissected were preserved. These smells accompanied Dr. Borodine's presence like the leitmotif of a Wagnerian hero. He was a tall man, slightly stooped, and although he could not have been more than forty at the time, he seemed already prematurely elderly. He moved around the laboratory in blue smock, here, peering at slides where paramecia were performing their swimmy stunts, there, shaking a mixture in a test tube and watching the color change. In his small kingdom he was alchemist-ruler. But he had a more romantic image for me. Boris Borodine had escaped from Russia, where he had been a student at the time of the Revolution — an early Menshevik upriser. When the Bolsheviks took over, he had been forced to flee, somehow finding his way here to the science laboratory of the Weston School. I could see him young, but looking much the same, with his elongated face, high forehead, long nose, thin neck with a prominent Adam's apple, and small gentle eyes. His baldness hidden by a rakish student's beret, he had been part of a mob shouting curses at the Czar and carrying angry placards in Kremlin Square. Dr. Borodine never spoke of his early days and I learned his story from others. It was difficult to imagine him in a crowd, part of a movement, because now he appeared very much a loner, at home in the company of his pickled frogs and wiggling paramecia. I appreciated his chivalrous absentminded manner, and although science was not my strong point, I spent as much time as possible in Dr. Borodine's laboratory, observing him with admiration tinged with compassion. I would pretend to be bending over an experiment, but all the time I would be watching his face. Sometimes when his eyes met mine, I would imagine I saw a slight contraction of the pupils, a minute squint, as though he were looking into the sun, and I would take this to be a symptom of reciprocated feeling. I treasured the look and only wished it were not so ephemeral — that I could preserve it like a four-leaf clover pressed between the pages of an album or the silver cartridge lipstick that had been at the bottom of my jewel box. I looked forward to school each day in the hope of one of those stray looks, and lacking that, the sight of Boris Borodine moving around the science laboratory in a blue smock, shy and patient, when his past had been colorful and dangerous, was quite enough for me.

On weekends, on some pretext, I would walk alone in the neighborhood of the apartment house where I knew he lived. It was located on a grubby side street where children played among the ash cans. There was a laundry, a liquor store, a cheap restaurant — and all these places were invested with special glamour. The building itself was new. A raw-red canopy bore the magic numbers: Two Twenty. I would peer inside but it was too dark to familiarize myself with the interior. I circled around and around the block, trying not to appear idle, but as though bent on urgent business. Sometimes my efforts were rewarded, and like a fisherman who at last feels a nibble on his line, I would run into Dr. Borodine. I would invariably appear surprised at the encounter, but oddly, he never did, as though bumping into me on the street were the most expected thing in his life. Later, after one of these successful expeditions, I would interpret this as meaning that he had been thinking of me as he walked, absentmindedly, his long neck bent forward, wearing a beret left over from his stormy student days at a jaunty angle.

"Good morning," he might say, his eyes squinting in that particular way. "What brings you to my neighborhood on this fine day?"

I felt sure he must know, and those words were just part of a game we both were playing. At any rate, I was always well satisfied by our meager dialogue and returned home as from a day's work well done.

Once Dr. Borodine was absent from school with a chest cold. Gathering my courage, I decided to leave a sympathetic note at his door. My wastepaper basket was filled with false starts before I settled for the final draft, in a studied handwriting not my own. When I reached his apartment house I hesitated at the entrance, not so much because of nervousness as to prolong the delight of anticipation. I realized that not only was I now to know that dark, faintly glimpsed lobby, but I would also ride up in the elevator Dr. Borodine used each day, see his landing, his door, ring his bell — and, perhaps, he might even invite me in. It was not outside the realm of possibility — only the step seemed far off, like the hazy adventures waiting for me in that fictitious time called the future! With my envelope in hand I entered at last. A superintendent in shirt sleeves was standing by the door.

"Dr. Boris Borodine," I said, savoring each syllable. "I have a letter for him. What is the number of his apartment?"

"Sorry, miss, he is on the twelfth floor, but the elevator is out of order. No one is allowed up. You can give me the letter. I will see that he gets it."

"No, thank you," I said, and retreated, but not before noticing, like a detective, that the lobby contained a large breakfront with a sparse collection of china plates. At the first ash can, I tore my letter into small bits and dropped it inside. My heart was pounding as from a narrow escape and my feet were leaden on the way home.

Mr. Gopal Chatterji and Dr. Boris Borodine, once so central in my daydreams, equally innocent of their respective roles, gradually faded away. Years later, I heard, almost without emotion, that Mr. Chatterji had hung himself on a bathroom hook and that Dr. Borodine had married a German history teacher, and together they were running a progressive boarding school on Long Island. The sage philosopher had been defeated, as had the outsized brave loner. But, perhaps, neither had ever really existed. It may be that both were creations of my imagination that have left stubborn traces, appearing and reappearing in different forms, at different ages, combined in one person, or separate, like the various shapes assumed by Jupiter when he descended from the sky to the earth in order to seduce some unsuspecting mortal.

Years later when I revisited the Weston School, the second floor was still familiar, yet somehow flat. In the alcove at the end of the hall, a vase of insipid artificial flowers had replaced the enigmatic Buddha that had once presided there.

From a distance Central Park is seen merely as a green ribbon bisecting the city canyon. But on close view, to a child growing up in New York City, it also represents many lands: the Sixtieth Street entrance, leading to the smelly, caged kingdom of the zoo; an echoing black tunnel; the steep incline named Donkey Hill (how diminished it looks now!), surmounted by the statue of a sled dog, Balto of

Nome; the forum of the mall; the grand stairs descending to a fountain from which rises a bronze angel, with a hazy lake in the background like a Leonardo da Vinci landscape; the Sailboat Pond; the flatland of Sheep's Meadow; and the unexplored woods uptown, once the queasy route to the Thomas Jefferson School.

For many years I would meet my park friends every afternoon, come wind and weather, at the mall. Every season had its special equipment: skates, hoops, bicycles, yo-yos, sleds. Each day we would follow the same imitation rural paths, newly budded, golden leaved, or blanketed in snow, to our convening place, presided over by the stern figures of the commemorated great on their marble pedestals. The mademoiselles sat on their same bench unraveling endless lengths of gossip about their *"patrons,"* interspersed with admonitions directed toward us. Mademoiselle Moeller, a chunky Swiss lady, belonged to *"les petits* Firbanks," consisting of Marjorie (my peer), Janet, next, Pauline, youngest, with a long-awaited heir, Reginald, in his baby carriage. Mademoiselle La Fond was a Parisian, brittle-thin, dressed in black, and, in my memory, always wearing pearl-gray spats. She was in charge of Denise McLeod, the exotic member of the clan, her mother being French and flighty — according to Mademoiselle La Fond, *"un mauvais sujet"* who danced until dawn (I saw her wearing gilt slippers and carrying a minute mesh purse) while her stockbroker husband worked hard all day to provide her with the frivolities she took for granted. Small wonder that Denise, an only child, was a problem! But to me she seemed delightful, dimpled, and fairylike, with an imaginative, inexhaustible repertory of misdemeanors, whereas the Firbanks were bland and virtuous. From Mademoiselle Moeller it was learned that their mother was years older than their physician father and had produced three grown daughters by her *"première noce."* This new family was *"un miracle,"* especially, *"le petit* Reggie."

My Central Park clan was as well known to me as the members of my own household, although we met only at the mall and learned about each other's families from overheard remarks issuing from the mademoiselles' bench. It was hard for me to imagine what my mademoiselle could have to say about my own uninteresting parents that could match the tales about "les Firbanks" and "les McLeods." I did see Dr. and Mrs. Firbank once at a birthday party for Marjorie. Although *"tellement plus jeune,"* he looked old and drab to me, and his wife proved to be an ordinary type no more senior than anyone else's mother. In the park one afternoon, I met Mrs. McLeod when she appeared to pick up Denise to pay a call. She too turned out to be a disappointment, her plump body squeezed into a tailored suit, lacking dancing slippers and the golden purse. Reality was too insignificant for remembrance and I still, automatically, think of the McLeods and the Firbanks as they were conjured up, through snatches of gossip, by three French-speaking weird sisters, sitting on a certain bench at the north end of the mall, until the day grew late and it was the hour to move homeward. We played intricate games, rode our bicycles or skated up and down the promenade, always recalled when we ventured toward the south, too far afield. Cousins and school friends who frequented different areas of the park were out of bounds. We never encountered them. They were foreigners, skating, bicycling, drawing hopscotches, and choosing teams, while their guardians also gossiped on benches situated at the Rambles, Donkey Hill, the Boat Pond, or Sheep's Meadow. On the mall, the familiars were often joined by other children. Their faces have blurred with time, but our games are still with me. I have only to hear the clatter of skates on asphalt or the treble shout "Not it!" to see again the past, as well preserved as the brocade costumes in glass cases in the museums in Europe. A game I particularly enjoyed was called "Statues." We would go through a series of fantastic poses, romantic or clownish, while one of us, with her back turned, would count to seven and call out, "Still Pond — No More Moving!" or some such incantation. With that, she would twirl around and the rest of us would have to freeze in the pose of the instant — the most bizarre being the winner — our flesh and blood gallery competing with the grave lifeless file of statues on the mall that were destined for limitless endurance.

In cold weather, the aroma of roasting chestnuts greets you at the entrance to Central Park at Sixtieth Street. When it is warm, the stagnant odor of animals in the zoo is overpowering. These smells and the soft plushy feeling of my beaver carriage cover make up my initial awareness of park life. My first years were a time for observation; the activities and social successes on the mall were reserved for the future. Reviewing those early memories of Central

Park, I find they have a unity, curiosity and recoil mingling in equal proportion. It seems to me that the jolly placid existence laid down for children is mainly an adult invention. The very young, mutely, in secret, are taking note of an underworld that unrolls around them like a half-understood film, full of fascination and horror. I can still see the hobos who used the park for their clubhouse. Lumpy shapes, wrapped in sacking, hugging a bottle, wearing large shoes torn and turned up at the toes, they seemed both cheerful and frivolous. But, later, the unemployed who sold apples on the other side of the wall looked dreary and peaked and, in my memory, their noses are perpetually red and dripping from the cold. Once, a man planted in a pile of fallen leaves looked me straight in the eyes, as with deliberation he opened his pants. His penis, pointing directly at me, was as imperious as a raised finger, and exposed to the shock of cold air, it looked hot, not frozen like the noses of the apple vendors nearby. These are the pictures that remain. The pony cart rides and the colorful balloons I know were there also, but I cannot see them anymore. The crowning episode of that old film was set at the zoo. I remember a crowd in front of the polar bear cage. The animal is mountainous and white, dancing for us on two legs and eating the peanuts he is offered with the self-conscious manners of a clown. Suddenly, a siren is heard, cutting like a knife through the familiar noises at the zoo. I am pushed back by the surging mob and, somehow, I absorb the information — although I do not witness the act — that the bear has bitten off the arm of a little girl. I do not see her, but I watch a covered stretcher being carried toward the waiting ambulance, and the crowd parts respectfully, as though a celebrity were passing by. Later, when the nurses chew over the event, I hear the girl's name. I think I know her. Although I never see her again, in my mind's eye, she is tall and very thin, with matching tweed coat, bonnet, and leggings — the park uniform. One arm is completely missing, like the long-limbed doll in my nursery, once new beneath the Christmas tree, since relegated to the disorderly interment of the toy box. Soon after that I made the move uptown, and the zoo, the ivy-covered police station, the tramps, and the memory of the accident were left behind. But the smell of roasting chestnuts, caged animals, and the wail of an ambulance siren can resurrect a film, still sensational and horrifying, though made so many years ago.

In my childhood, Central Park was unknown to me at night. Like a magic carpet, it was rolled up and stored at sundown, to be spread out once more for my use in the daylight hours. It was not until adolescence that it emerged in evening apparel. But memory has little use for later images, as the scarcity and brightness of childhood impressions has been replaced by the passage of time, by a multiplicity of recollections, many of them blurred and marred by their proximity to the present day, so that I am forced to test, select, and discard. It seems to me that during adolescence I never saw the park spread out before me, but only glimpsed it in small, jagged pieces, like the parts of a jigsaw puzzle. I see myself in a taxi on the way home from a dance during the Christmas holidays. Their approach was long and ceremonious and their duration so short that in January, when the Christmas trees lay rejected on the streets with bits of tinsel still clinging to them like silver tears, I had the feeling that none of it had actually taken place. It was all a dream, summoned one cold snowy night. The ritual began with shopping for evening dresses with my mother. There must have been one for each event of the vacation — beautiful and shimmering for one night and evanescent like the brief life span of a butterfly. Yet I can recall each one separately: the red velvet, decorous and traditional; the peacock blue with the bustle, coy and frivolous; the black taffeta with its flounced skirt, a flamenco dancer; and the white net, trimmed in silver kid, as shining as the Christmas tree star itself. They were personalities in themselves and, in my memory, they seem to stand without me. But once inside one of them, I faced the world remade, each night a new victor. My mother, so simple in her own tastes and wishes, enjoyed decking me out with this lavishness. I see the dress shops, multiple-mirrored, my reflection thrown back at me from every angle and my mother sitting quietly by, her own beauty subordinated by her humble role, like a stage mother waiting in the wings. In retrospect, I marvel at those strange puberty rites — this expensive, wasteful method for snaring the opposite sex — so many bejeweled traps, when the catch, I am certain, would have glided just as easily into an ordinary unadorned fishnet. On the way back from the party, the pristine gauzy dress, so carefully handled on the way out, was forgotten in the crush of postponed embraces in the dark of an overheated taxi. Over one tuxedoed shoulder, I sometimes noted through the back window a segment of the park, heartbreakingly beautiful in crusty, sparkling snow, rimmed by the lighted towers of Central Park South — a moonstone sunk deeply in a many-faceted setting. I wanted to absorb all of it — to halt right here. But the insistent, dark embrace was powerful, and its warm blackness could obliterate the sparkling cold outside. And the white dress, with its silver leather trimming, the product of so many hours of careful collaboration by my mother, the saleswoman, and me, was crushed, twisted, and torn, utterly disregarded in the heedless hunger of the moment.

Nowadays I find that Central Park has dwindled. With my large black poodle pulling me on, it is possible to cross the well-known land from the mall to the Sixtieth Street entrance in the space of a few minutes. Yet the terrain is unaltered, only the cast of characters has changed. I no longer see the mademoiselles lined up on benches like chattering sparrows along telegraph wires, the hobos, and the shabby army of unemployed. Even the breed of dogs is different, poodles, Afghans, and basset hounds having replaced the fox terriers, Pekingese, and chows of my childhood. True, an occasional infant's nurse in white spongy shoes is still found pushing the eternal English "pram"; schoolchildren in uniform, with scabby knees, are still playing games of ball; the same squirrels still regard me with shy, bright, eager eyes; and the horses and buggies, garlanded and rickety, with their antique drivers, still clatter around the park, preserved in an elixir of timelessness. These are the only remains, and I, an observer once more, am watching a new film on the old set. But the present is a transparency laid over the obtruding past.

On the mall, I have moved among groups of young people demonstrating against the Vietnam war. I am with them in their protest, but I am excluded from their rites. Invisible, I pass through the crowd. I note that in spite of the grimness of the plea, the scene has a festive air, like a children's party. The placards proclaiming "Make Love, Not War" have a homemade look, like party favors. The costumes are fanciful; long hair floats over capes and fringed Indian shawls. Beaded necklaces and headbands remind me of the trinkets extracted from the paper snappers after their sparks have been exploded. Across the drive, around the fountain basin, guarded by the spread angel wings, hippies often gathered for music sessions. Herded closely, as though body proximity were communication, they compose a moving mosaic. A small band is separated from the rest — shocking pink and purple battered felt hats, black faces, under huge puffy black halos, long matted manes hanging lankly around sad white faces. The music sounds sad too, with a hint of menace, noisy and rhythmic. And I do not recognize the instruments. I find myself a stranger in a strange world.

But is it so much more alien than my own past? I seem to have been moved along on an escalator while remaining motionless, and from the present, I survey that round-eyed baby under the fur robe, that busy citizen of the mall playing her important games, the mindless white and silver apparition in the closeness of a taxi on a winter's night. And where are the crowds of anxious young mothers, watching over their children in the snug meeting places around the Sailboat Pond, while young husbands, remembered in new resplendent uniforms, have disappeared to far-flung places to fight another world war? What has become of that handsome well-dressed couple, verging on middle age, who met in the park long ago, their bodies straining eagerly toward each other as though against a high wind, their arms raised in a greeting that resembled a farewell? Instead, I see two dazed young people sitting side by side. I know that the cigarette stub they are sharing is marijuana, passed from hand to hand, like the peace pipe of old. Inside a hansom cab, another pair is tangled together, long hair enmeshed in long hair, four wide trouser legs entwined. Which is boy? Which is girl? Yet the swirling embrace has the romantic grace of an art nouveau poster.

Everywhere, at short view, the characters in Central Park are new, arrested before my eyes in fantastic poses, like the shapes assumed in the game of Statues I used to play with my friends on the mall. *One, two, three, four, five, six, seven — Still Pond — No More Moving!* But they too will not hold their positions long. What will they be in ten years' time? Twenty? Like me, they are being moved along. And in the long view, is it not possible that the differences are more apparent than real? Once, in Central Park, my grandmother, Hannah Frank, went driving, the gray plume in her hat proclaiming, seemingly forever, her state of formal semimourning. In a hansom cab, my father, nervous, with damp palms, proposed to my mother. And here, my many selves disported themselves and disappeared — as will my present one, led on by a black poodle — and all these mountebank children, too. Around and around the generations circle, differently disguised but with an underlying sameness, like the horses in their various gaudy caparisons, vanishing and returning as they spin inside the carousel I used to ride in the park so many lives ago.

CHAPTER V

AFTER MY MOTHER'S DEATH MY FATHER CONCENTRATED his belongings mainly in the modest confines of his "dressing room." Here all the relics from the past were crowded like the collection of a fusty museum. His bed looked big, out of place. But the cretonne-upholstered sofa (with its clinical mechanical device for raising and lowering) was the same my mother used to use — where I would find her stretched out, blue-veined and pale, warmed only by the small flames of her amber necklace, on my return from school. When my father rested there at the end of the day, it lost its sepulchral look and he would appear comfortable and padded in his bathrobe, with his ankles encased in the long underwear he always wore winter and summer and his feet in gray carpet slippers sticking out from under the couch throw. His afternoon nap was a well-defined postscript to his day, a prelude to dinner in a restaurant, a concert, theater, while my mother's rest was a flight from worry, a journey without definite limits, a rehearsal for death.

The painting of the German beer hall that used to be in my grandfather's apartment had found its way to my father's dressing room. With its carved gilt frame, it looked too heavy for the wall and it seemed a miracle that it never tumbled down upon the couch beneath it. Although oversized in my father's dressing room, the painting had lost its depth. I no longer entered another world through its dark oily surface. Only the bright white, unprinted, unfinished newspaper still caught my eye. At the head of my father's bed was the Velázquez reproduction, the same that had divided the honors with the player piano in the foyer of that first apartment where I was born. No one looked at it anymore. On either side of the mirror over the bureau were the portraits of my grandparents taken by the photographer who had shared my father's bachelor flat many years before. Though lacking color, my grandfather's image was as I remembered it: square-faced, square-bearded, with a fair ponderous aspect like the King of Hearts in a pack of cards. But old age was not becoming to my grandmother. Although my father always described her as small, pert, and sparkling, her face appeared gross and plain, with a thickened nose and small intelligent eyes that reminded me of my father's. But I viewed them with neither recognition nor reassurance. These photographs hung in their places like set altar pieces, an accepted gesture to filial piety.

Before lying down on his sofa my father always emptied the contents of his pockets upon the bureau. These too were part of the museum, like bits of jewelry and artifacts from bygone eras, uninteresting in themselves but necessary to complete the collection. There was a considerable amount of paper money, crumpled and casually scattered; the black-

and silver-checkerboard knife, a long-ago birthday gift from me; the thick old-fashioned watch, chain, and onyx fob that had belonged to my grandfather; the gold pencil (found by my father among my mother's things after her death), intended for his sixty-eighth birthday a week later. His pockets also disgorged bits of exotic candy, licorice, coconut, marzipan, which he bought in Yorkville. They were descendants of the sweets enjoyed by my father and his cousins after school in the Brooklyn brewery yard. Tickets for a concert or theater would be stuck jauntily in the frame of the mirror, reminders of an extravagant evening ahead. On the bedside table stood my mother's familiar bridal picture and a photograph of my brother and me, aged about six and eight. He is dressed in a sailor suit, blond and pretty, but with an uneasy look in his eyes, something vaguely unfortunate rather than unhappy — I, round-faced, round-eyed, and solemn, with dark straight bangs and strangely long-fingered babyish hands folded on my lap.

From this room my father would emerge every day, freshly shaved and showered, his brown face exuding a kind of understated health that one felt would endure longer than the rosy exuberant variety. And he would be ready to start for the brewery. Sometime between the repeal of Prohibition and the death of his engineering partner, Walter Keogh, my father entered the family concern in Brooklyn. At the period following my mother's death, it had become as much a source of renewal and consolation for him as it had been for so many years for his brother Carl. Somehow, by what tactics I was never told, my father, younger brother and latecomer, took over the reins of the business, while Uncle Carl, good-natured and self-effacing, stepped down. But it was Carl who still seemed to embody the old traditions. Sampling beer like a true German brewmaster, he seemed closer to the original Ludwigsburg brewer, while my father was the link with newer days, the world of improved machinery, modern advertising, and reconstruction.

But as he grew older, he too seemed to be turning his eyes toward the past. Some mornings following the death of my mother, I would accompany him on the drive from New York City to Brooklyn. Along the way he took pleasure in telling me anecdotes from his boyhood in Bushwick and the historical past in Ludwigsburg. I listened patiently but without much interest. I was glad to distract him from his sorrow and also to prevent him from reminiscing about my mother, which always embarrassed me and gave me a queasy feeling of insecurity. Grief seemed foreign to my father and my presence was there to prevent it. Also his nearness could still dispel the metaphysical jimjams, gone for many years but hovering over me again after my mother's sudden death. The old incantation had altered. *Who am I? I am nothing, come from nothing, going to nothing . . .* had become *she was here, she has gone, I am here, I will go* — but it was essentially the same refrain, thrillingly, terrifyingly familiar, still empowered to overwhelm me and to obliterate all else, even sorrow. Now looking back, I realize how lonely my father must have been, barred from mourning by someone close to him and to her. But perhaps, physical proximity, not words, strengthens family ties and, possibly, my father with his earthy wisdom understood this better than I.

With the passage of time, I detect a repetitive pattern in the generations. On those Sunday morning visits to my grandfather, it was I, a child, who was avidly attentive to tales from the past, while the thoughts of my father were elsewhere as he waited absently for the visit's end. Now the past was meaningful to him and it was my turn to be somewhat bored and restive. It is true that there is a bond between childhood and age. The former is an empty beach, waiting for the incoming tide, and the remains of the undersea world form interesting mosaiclike designs in the sand. The latter is a beach from which the tide is receding, once again uncovering submerged treasure, while middle life represents the seashore at high tide. It is carnival time: the patterns in the sand created at a different hour are hidden and the bustling crowd is too noisy to heed the inexorable crashing of the waves nearby.

The drive to Brooklyn was an ugly assault. Through the windows of the car, row after row of small identical red brick houses moved past us, expressionless and bare, poverty without individuality, newness without hope. I felt uncomfortable on the back seat under the lap robe with my father, while Kevin, his chauffeur for many years, drove us proudly to the accustomed destination as if he owned the territory along the way. At times the miles of housing development would give way to acres of cemetery, where the anonymous slabs were interspersed with grotesque angel wings, black wreaths, obelisks, and temples, as though the possibility of differentiation in dwelling place were reserved for those beneath the earth rather than for those living above it.

The sordid drive did not seem to bother my father because it was the way to his generalship at the brewery. He even pointed out the latest housing development with something of the same zest he used to show on our sightseeing expeditions abroad. World War II had turned these into ancient history. Europe, the vacation land, had become a deadly volcano, and was so depicted in the United States in the papers and the newsreel theaters, where it was accompanied by the commentator's bland, unsurprised voice. Also my own family, my husband newly an officer in the navy and my infant son, divided my life from those past times as finally as world events were separating us all from the Europe of a year or two before.

"Look, on the right is the new bottling plant." My father's voice was still pointing out the sights to me. But now we had arrived at the brewery.

My father and Uncle Carl sat at old-fashioned twin rolltop desks pushed back to back. Facing one another but hidden by their tall desks, the brothers looked like some kind of two-headed allegorical animal. Their office remained traditional but change was encroaching all around them. Next door my brother, in charge of advertising, operated from a room directly out of the pages of *House Beautiful*. Flowered chintz, fragile china, English furniture camouflaged the manufacture of beer, like sugar coating on a pill. His office also displayed colored photographs of models who had sung the praises of Rheingold beer from a succession of perfect painted lips: under floppy straw hats in summer, ermine-hooded in winter, carrying flowers, ski poles, parasols, basking in sunlight, moonlight, ducking April showers, pastoral, urban — but everywhere and always enthusiastic about the golden frothy inimitable unmistakable Kupperman brew. Uncle Carl would squint, perplexed at those lustrous beauties, in the same way that he watched the construction of the new streamlined buildings and ramps sleek in glass and steel. He was admiring but uncomprehending and a little sad, while my father was enthusiastic, and though he and my brother Nicholas bickered over details, they were in essential agreement that in business to stand still is to die.

In the lunchroom I surveyed the remains of the Kupperman clan. They appeared a straggling group, thinned out by the smaller families of contemporary times and absences made by the war. Also, it seemed to me that they eyed one another with distrust. Their manner was obsequious toward my father, but an undercurrent of envy and dislike was directed to his son and heir. Nicholas had changed radically since the photograph taken in his sailor suit. He was unnaturally tall and prematurely stooped. His nose had grown large, high-bridged, and only his eyes were the same, uneasy and vaguely wild. His huge awkward person was an almost comic contrast to his small trim father whose subtle strength was needed to bolster Nicholas' sprawling energies. Surveying the family and the ancestral portraits, it occurred to me that Nicholas was not a Kupperman at all. Perhaps his tall stooped silhouette harked back to Isaac Frank, the long-dead, towering master of the house on Sixty-second Street.

When the German cook appeared with a steaming pot of stew, the fragrance that enveloped the lunch table had a unifying effect — rich, meaty, dark brown — veal, venison or hare — the smell could have issued straight from the kitchen in Ludwigsburg. This aroma and the tall glasses of beer, cold but not overchilled, with just the right size crown of foam, the pride of Uncle Carl, seemed to proclaim the continuing reign of the Kuppermans within a changing scene. But one new person sat near the head of the table: Dr. Hermann Walden, representative of the La Rivières, recent partners of the Kuppermans. He was short and fat, squeezed into his skin like a German sausage, with a naked bullet head and heavy blue eyes that I mistrusted. Although I did not know it then, his presence, like a single alien malignant cell in the bloodstream, was to be a warrant of death for the Kupperman Breweries.

My introduction to Dr. Walden and the La Rivières was in 1939, a year that marked an end and a beginning, though at the time I was taken largely unawares and the world around me seemed to be wrapped in ignorant dreams. It was spring, and I remember being on board a shining white yacht that my father had chartered. We were heading across Long Island Sound toward the World's Fair. The picture is very distant; it appears further away than my childhood and the passengers are so faded I can barely see them. Sometimes now, on my way to the airport, when I catch a dart of light from the shallow marshy water streaking the Long Island flats, or when I see the huge useless globe left over from the fair, like a toy abandoned by an infant giant, the yachting party returns to me for an instant, a wavering image. And I recall the falsely festive mood of that afternoon, the galvanized effort to enjoy. This spirit was reflected in the greater world by the fair, a monster playground where Money, Novelty, Technocracy, Culture disported themselves like gargantuan nymphs whose bulk blotted out the gathering storm clouds. I see the obelisk, the perisphere, miles of glass, concrete arcades, vistas, the pavilions of Russia, France, Germany, India, Switzerland, Japan, etc., competing during long sunny days and neon-lighted nights.

As we sat on the boat, my father, as host, was the central figure. Although still stunned by my mother's death the year before, now at sixty-nine, with his irrepressible will to live, he was attempting to return to the pleasures of his bachelor days. Outwardly it was all there: the spruce yacht, the guests, and he, in white flannels, blue blazer, and Panama hat. But in spite of his valiant effort, it seemed to me that this boating party had a hollow note, a feeling of failure. As we steamed over the Sound, our group mirrored the fair's opulent falseness. The company was composed of my husband, my brother, myself, a cool blond divorcée, an emigré Austrian prince and princess, pallid copies of a vanished world, and members of the La Rivière family. There were Eugene, René, his brother, and the next generation represented by René's son Christian, also Dr. Hermann Walden, brewmaster from Berlin, Walden's wife Lisa, and their daughter Charlotte.

The La Rivières were of French origin but they had emigrated to the Argentine, remaining there for several generations. They had recently returned to Paris when their great wealth was threatened in South America. Breweries were among their holdings in many parts of the world, and now, Rheingold, the sole possession of the Kuppermans, had been added to their empire. I don't know the exact moment of the appearance of the La Rivières in my father's life. The years shrink and become indistinguishable. But by the time he took over the business, the snug world inside the brewery yard had long since disappeared. Competition and rivalry, inside and out, dissension and envy flourished. But my father, like a minor Napoleon, set out to subdue it all. He even imagined, like many a vigorous man before him, that after his death he would still be able to reach out from the grave to arrange things his way. In order to insure the succession of his son, he introduced a foreign element into the midst of the bickering Kuppermans. Fifty-one percent of the business was sold to the La Rivières with the understanding that the running of the brewery would be left to my father but in case of open civil war and a possible overthrow of his personal dynasty, they could be counted on to vote on his side. My father was well satisfied with his coup and proud of his association with the La Rivières. He often referred to them as "swells" — a term I detested, meaning to me that they were aristocrats, we bourgeois, they cosmopolites, we from Brooklyn, they fabulously wealthy, we solidly so — and worst of all, they Christian, we Jewish. Although my father's manner to them was that of a cordial host and they treated him with polite respect and even that touch of deference due from dilettantes to a man of action, no matter how circumscribed his field, the La Rivières brought back again that feeling of mild shame I experienced when I remembered the time, so many years ago, when we were living at Green Meadows and I watched my parents, like good vassals, preparing to visit the Rothburgs at the top of the hill.

I studied the La Rivières as they sat on the deck of the yacht. Eugene and René were middle-aged, much alike, with neat gray mustaches. Eugene wore a monocle and they both had worried eyes. Their wealth weighed on them like a relentless incubus. It was said that in their anxiety they had buried gold brick in several corners of the world. Eugene clasped his bony hands as though in prayer and René's nose twitched. Only young Christian appeared to be free from the burden. He was volatile and handsome like a black butterfly poised on the verge of flight. Dr. Walden was both groveling and arrogant and he had about him a sinister air of intrigue, a diplomat in beer. His wife and daughter had carefully coifed hair and were overdressed and coarse. Lisa, the wife, was timid and apologetic, while Charlotte was confident and acted as though she were married to Dr. Walden. Father and daughter had the same heavy blue eyes, mutely sharing some secret. Perhaps they were dreaming together of the buried bricks of gold like a pirate's treasure that belonged to their masters, the La Rivières.

Arriving at the fair, our party set out for Rheingold Village, a replica of a German town. We sat around a table covered by a red- and white-checked cloth, beside a trellis entwined with artificial vines, and were served by waiters in native costume. We drank beer from stone mugs, but only Dr. Walden seemed to be enjoying himself as he sipped, paused judiciously, and sipped again and pondered the quality of the brew. *"Prosit,"* he toasted, touching his stein dexterously to the others. As for me, this cardboard evocation of Ludwigsburg was depressing. The village existing in my imagination had been rendered only too real by this commercial display. Or was it simply that I had lost my interest in the past? At any rate, the setting was offensive, as distasteful as an old lady who should have been staying home with her memories, but who paraded into the world, brazenly painted, posturing as a girl and going through the gestures of her flirtatious youth. Also, for all of us, the Germany of beer gardens, *lederhosen,* and medieval clock towers was no more. In its place armored tanks, goose-stepping files of soldiers, and a ranting madman were advancing on the rest of Europe. Yet we sat on at Rheingold Village, pretending to enjoy ourselves as we listened to Viennese waltzes and praised the bratwurst and sauerkraut while the fair whirled around us and beyond it: the world was moving steadily toward war.

This scene fades out quickly and the group around the brewery lunch table also, to be called up again inadvertently at the sight of glinting water on the Long Island flats or by the savory smell of stew —

But the threshold of my father's room and his stepping across it on his way to work in the morning — or in the evening, bent on enjoying his favorite restaurant after he and Kevin had called for some lady companion — these moments I can still imagine at will.

My father outlived my mother by almost twenty years, an odd reversal of the expected, since he was eleven years her senior and she, with her characteristic anxiety, had worried, long in advance, how she would cope with the brutal, dangerous world when he was gone. I remember from my childhood a special phrase whistled by one parent when looking for the other. I never knew its origin but its one sustained note followed by three in rapid succession remain with me to this day, and I see my mother's face flooded with relief at my father's whistle answering hers. It might have been at the sound of his latchkey in the front door, at the usual hour of his return home in the evening, or he could have been only in the adjoining room, but her disproportionate emotion would have been more suitable to the reunion of Orpheus and Eurydice. My mother could not have endured her whistle to have remained unanswered. But the card that we are expecting is the one that is rarely dealt to us, and it was my father who lived on alone. It was certainly better that way. And although he undoubtedly experienced many moments of loneliness and loss, I am sure that life tasted good to him almost to the end. My father held firmly to many pleasures in his descent into old age. He remained an enthusiastic, energetic traveler; he enjoyed good food, wine, and pretty women. He still visited the Metropolitan

Museum (now generally unaccompanied) and continued his brisk walks to survey the grandeurs of the past and the bold constructions of the future. But the keystone of his way of life, a condition he clung to with almost superstitious fervor, was that he must never, under any circumstance, be obliged to spend an evening by himself. And I do believe, with the help of Daisy Heinz, he never did. When his family or the younger more glamorous women he knew failed him, he could always count on her.

Daisy Heinz was attached to our family history for more than half a century. Yet she never seemed related to us — just there — like a single asparagus seed blown from the field into a flower garden border. She was the tough slender stalk reappearing incongruously through the years, coexisting with its dissimilar neighbors while retaining its own jaunty, resilient, slightly obscene individuality.

The last time I saw her was in a city hospital ward. A friend from her apartment house had telephoned to say that Daisy's son had committed her after she had fractured her hip in a fall. As I walked in that unfamiliar part of town, I admit that my thoughts were more on the anticipated horrors I was about to see than on Daisy herself. The hospital building did nothing to reassure me — old stone the color of dry blood and small windows like a prison. It was set in a meager grass plot dotted with benches. I observed the people seated at ease, seemingly oblivious to their ominous surroundings. As they basked in the early spring sunshine, they might have been vacationers on an esplanade waiting for the band concert to begin. I could not tell whether they were employees or inmates of that hideous building, but I thought I caught sight of a pajama leg, or perhaps it was only a white uniform, as I hurried past.

Inside I was assailed by the smell of hospitals, an amalgam of brass polish, disinfectant, ether, and linoleum. Consulting my notes like a lone traveler, I asked directions to Daisy's ward. As the elevator rose, I tried not to look at the stretcher crowding me against the wall. But out of the corner of my eye, I could not help seeing a construction of tubes and bottles surrounding a mound that passed for an ordinary citizen in this nightmare land. Daisy's door was at the end of a long corridor and when I entered, I almost lost heart and bolted. Where in this maze of iron cots, here and there separated by flimsy screens, would I find her? Would I be obliged to scrutinize each tortured face until I recognized hers? I was standing uncertainly at the entrance when a familiar voice from a bed nearly called out, "Hi, there, come in and park your chassis."

It was Daisy, unmistakably, and that vocabulary was peculiarly hers. But it issued from a skeleton. Daisy's face was as reduced as an African shrunken head framed by two tiny white braids, and her arm raised in greeting was a winter twig. But for that jaunty command, I would not have believed her identity. I sat down at her side and we began to talk — I, with considerable constraint, still trying not to see the other patients, who seemed to be eyeing me with curiosity from behind their bars and wire attachments; she, with avidity, as though slaking a long thirst. Mostly we spoke of my father. We seemed to be referring to two different people, but in an effort to cheer her, I tried to fit my image of him to hers, like a trained nurse keeping pace with a charge. Although I hadn't seen Daisy since my father's death, her care had been left to my brother and me by his will.

"He always knew his way around," Daisy was saying. "I can tell you, at the Colony restaurant, he never had to wait for a table — he was a saint about my boys. It was never necessary to ask him twice — that last summer abroad he and I lived like royalty on Lake Como —"

It was a shame to interrupt her flow of reminiscences, which seemed to revive her like the champagne of the after-theater suppers of her youth. But it was time to discuss practical matters, and besides, I was in a hurry to get away before those disembodied eyes and rigged shapes lost their blur and turned into a suffering human being.

"Daisy," I said softly but firmly, "I'm going to make arrangements to have you transferred to a nursing home."

"I won't go. I am going back to my apartment. It's just that Mona" (Daisy's daughter-in-law) "wants to put me out. She has always wanted to grab it for herself. She is a bad egg. My neighbors will take care of me. Mona is rotten and Tom is weak and sick again. He can't say no."

"But, Daisy, you won't be able to live alone until your hip mends." I was speaking sweetly, reasonably, to the embattled, courageous remains on the bed, while all the while I was controlling my own helpless panic and desire to run away before the sights and smells of that place could overcome me.

Suddenly, she capitulated, as with the jauntiness of her greeting she raised her little claw again in a theatrical gesture of assent. "O.K. Look who's the boss lady."

Gratefully receiving my exit cue, I fled.

I have pieced together her story and now a whole has evolved that is probably more real than true. Agatha Peterson, as she was called then, was born in the Middle West in the last part of the nineteenth century. Her mother had been one of the first women doctors in the country. I see her driving a gig over the flat lonely land to visit a patient in an isolated farmhouse. She would be wearing a poke bonnet and beneath it her face appeared, looking the way I remembered Daisy in her old age — catlike, snub-nosed, with a small determined mouth — but hers would be scrubbed clean, her lips rough from exposure to sun and wind, while Daisy's was always smudged by her lipstick gone awry. I see Daisy (Agatha), a dolllike figure in the gig beside her mother, accompanying her on her rounds. And I imagine her while she waited outside an impoverished farmhouse, vowing to herself that her life would not be played out against this drab background. No, she would push her way out, certain that there was something better ahead.

After that there's a blank space. When next I see Daisy Peterson (now no longer Agatha), she is on the stage of a New York City theater. The prairie provincial has evolved into a Ziegfield Follies girl. The Ziegfield girls appear to me like a combined finishing school and whorehouse. I picture their long-legged American Beauty nudity trimmed in feathers, ermine, bubbles, and spangles. I see them slowly, sinuously, descending stage ramps with the assurance of self-conscious sex, each one offering herself like a single jewel, yet part of a whole, a corps d'esprit out to conquer the male world. On tour, they crowd into plushy Pullman cars, giggling and chattering, smothered in floral offerings from admirers at points of departure and arrival. Like boarding-school girls, they speak a special language, and Daisy retained some of it to her dying day. She must have found it an exhilarating life, but I am sure that as she pinned on her picture hat before some backstage dressing room mirror and surveyed her hour-glass Edwardian image, she was confident that all this was just a step toward something even better ahead.

Then I see two young men in evening clothes presenting themselves at the Ziegfield Theatre stage door. They are my father and Harry Heinz. Harry had been my father's class-mate at the School of Mines and was an architect well on his way to success, specializing in the designing of New York City theaters. He was handsome in a bold reckless way and after a brief headlong courtship, it was he who placed a respectable gold band on Daisy's finger and the stage door closed behind her forever.

Daisy's faith at this period of her life must have been severely taxed. She had two infant sons and Harry still had the reputation for being a promising architect, but he was erratic, plagued by drink and drugs, frequently hospitalized for long stretches of time. It was my father who came to the rescue. He was at Daisy's side in the waiting room after baby Jack had swallowed a whistle in the middle of the night. It was his financial help that saw her through the fallow periods when Harry was incapable of constructing another theater. And maybe they started a love affair at this time, although that has always remained shrouded in Victorian secrecy. At any rate, it was the beginning of Daisy's lifelong devotion to my father. But eventually he married and although the assistance continued, the personal relationship receded. One summer, Tom, Daisy's youngest son, accompanied us to Europe as my brother's tutor. He was good-looking in an unsubstantial fashion and he lasted with us for about six weeks. Then after a hushed scene behind the closed doors of a hotel salon in Carlsbad, he was abruptly shipped back to the United States. My brother and I did not miss him, nor were we pleased by his departure. We were mainly curious about the cause and plagued Mademoiselle and our parents during tedious walks and long hotel meals. But all remained vague. I have the impression that he stole, committed some dishonest act, because always after, Tom's name was associated with such words as "congenital liar," "brilliant but unsound," and his image has remained tainted in my memory, as though he had inherited an unmentionable social disease from his wild, drunken, drug-addicted father.

Harry Heinz I saw only once. For some unremembered reason we were all driving into the country. He stands out in my memory, tall, white-haired, dressed all in black, with rimless glasses on a long black ribbon. He looked distinguished but ramshackle and his furrowed face twitched unremittingly, tirelessly. He reminded me of a judge or a diplomat, and it didn't seem possible that he was the creator of all those gilded, velvety theaters I visited on the occasions of birthday matinées.

Saturday afternoon matinées were celebration rituals when I was a child. A group of little girls in party dresses, shepherded by governesses or parents, were driven after a birthday luncheon eaten in broad daylight to the exciting, false evening light of a theater auditorium. Shivering with anticipation, we waited for the pretend world (soon to become more real than life outside) to begin, as the gold or red curtain rose and the crystal chandeliers began to dim. We would voluptuously consume candy from our party-favor boxes, and its stickiness blended with the candy-box sweetness of the theater, arabesques garlanding the stalls like icing on a wedding cake, on the ceiling floating-island clouds that pillowed succulent cherubs, and everywhere the raspberry-red of carpeting and seat upholstery.

At these times I experienced a distinguished surge of pride because my father had told me that his friend, Harry Heinz, had built almost every theater in New York City. The play might be a lavish musical, an historical drama with Essex bending low before a peppery Queen Elizabeth, a children's classic such as *Peter Pan* or *The Blue Bird* — it was all equally spellbinding, accompanied by the taste of fruit balls, peppermint, and chocolate kisses.

When the curtain fell and the lights went up for the final time, we were hurried into our Sunday coats and hats and herded up the aisle. I would take a last, long, loving look at the theater before receiving the shocking unreality of fresh air and the city afternoon outside.

In this way, Harry Heinz, seen only once, assumed a certain importance for me. One day I overheard my father telling my mother that "poor old Harry died at last." Yet Daisy remained hidden until my mother's death. Sometimes in the evening, in the library's cozy circle of lamplight, my father might remark, "Jack lost his job again. I think I'll have to find him a position at the brewery," or "Tom was taken to the hospital, unconscious. The doctors can't diagnose the trouble. Mona and the baby were evicted and have moved in with Daisy —" My mother would listen with that stricken look on her face that other people's troubles could always evoke. My father appeared unshaken, but I am sure that some of his day was given to Daisy when she was in trouble and called for his help.

Daisy's family tragedies swelled to grotesque proportions through the years. From their father, her sons had inherited drink, drugs, and an erratic brilliance, but Daisy's sturdy midwestern genes must have been recessive. After her removal to a nursing home in the country, the family catastrophies reached her more faintly. My brother and I provided her little room with a television set and a radio, and I liked to think that she had a pleasant outlook on trees and fields. I was told by the matter-of-fact matron that Daisy refused to mingle with the other patients but sat in her wheelchair all day alone. I do not think that she was dreaming of the past because, for Daisy, the next step still promised to be better. At some point during the trials of her life, she had become a Catholic convert, so I believe she was concentrating on the rewards of Heaven, now not far off. But in my mind's eye, Daisy's heaven is represented in sticky gold and red velvet, illumined by the stirring artificial night light of a theater visited long ago.

. .

The library in our apartment was a sliver of a room located between the dressing room and the living room. It was painted doctor's-office green — I had heard somewhere that green was supposed to stimulate the intelligence. Along one wall was a mahogany breakfront with glass doors facing the opposite wall covered by built-in bookshelves. Both sides looked equally immovable. Much of the furniture had come from that other apartment a few blocks south along Park Avenue. But to me it was a different world. We do not move as finally in space as we do in time, and that original home, the geography of my first eight years, might just as well have been an abandoned country, and I an émigré, who was never to return. Now both places have been deserted. But unlike my grandfather's apartment, they have not been torn down. They still stand, and when I glance inside their lobbies from the street, I am startled to discover, in apparently frozen attitudes, the brass-buttoned attendants of my childhood.

The "music room" at number 525 had evolved into the library at number 885. The grand piano had found its way into the living room and the portrait of the infant Bessie had vanished. The library was dominated by a towering engraving of Notre Dame framed in imitation of a Gothic portal, with the wide base flattened to look like a sidewalk. It had a monstrous immediacy. And it sometimes happened that when I found myself in the presence of the actual cathedral, it would appear remote — a picture postcard of itself — while the real thing was hanging ponderously, intimately, over the library sofa.

The crammed shelves of the breakfront and the bookcases opened this undistinguished room to many worlds. It was mainly my mother's collection; my father's reading consisted, for the most part, of the newspaper and "looking up" things in the *Encyclopaedia Britannica.* I was left free to browse, and sometimes now I am envious of the more catholic tastes of those years. I read in a disorderly, hungry way. I no longer remember at what time which book entered my life. The breakfront housed sets of Hardy, Meredith, Scott, Carlyle, George Eliot, Tennyson, and Mark Twain. At some point I tasted all of them. I am sure my understanding was incomplete but my absorption was nonetheless intense. The world beyond the library was large, indistinct, bland on the surface, but with lurking menace, like a garden in the dark. And books had the power to uncover unexplored areas, isolating them from the whole, as the light of a flashlight illumines for a moment a piece of syringa bush, the garden steps, a section of gravel path, turning each one into a never-before-seen microcosm, as finely detailed as a mosaic terrazzo, independent from the rest of the dusky garden.

The open shelves held a miscellany of books even more fascinating than the homogeneity of the sets. Children's classics stood cover to cover with Sinclair Lewis, Katherine

Mansfield, Sigrid Undset, and such wicked fare as Isadora Duncan's *My Life* and Radcliffe Hall's *The Well of Loneliness.* The text of *Peter Pan, Grimm's Fairy-Tales,* and *The Wind in the Willows* was accompanied by exotic illustrations on glossy paper protected by veils of transparent tracing paper. My mother's *Alice in Wonderland,* the same volume that had been presented to her on that blizzardy eighth birthday, was relocated here. I think I enjoyed my fantasies about the legendary Frank family (invoked by Pappa's spidery inscription on the flyleaf) more than the polite grotesqueries of Lewis Carroll. Isadora Duncan's autobiography and the half-understood pages of *The Well of Loneliness* would send premonitory thrills along my spine. I would read them furtively, alerted to footsteps. Since they had been candidly placed within my reach, perhaps there was no need for guilt, but that was part of pleasure, voluptuously not to be denied.

On occasional Thursday afternoons, Mademoiselle's day out, Kevin would drive my mother and me down Fifth Avenue to Brentano's. I often returned home with some prize like *Lad, A Dog* or *Nobody's Girl,* which would eventually find its way to the nursery shelves next to the *Bibliothèque rose,* the historical romances of Dumas, *Winnie the Pooh,* and *Little Women.* I made no distinction, I never compared. I remember the special smell of Brentano's, the infinite promise of the stacked books and the oil painting at the base of the stairs of a life-size woman in a red dress, one arm raised triumphantly, brandishing a book. She reminded me of the Statue of Liberty. Not long ago, in a bookstore on the Rue de Rivoli, the smell of new paper brought back those visits with all their original excitement. But either I had read the titles or they looked unpromising because I left empty-handed.

At the bottom of the library shelves, in a cabinet, were two large albums, one pink, one blue, entitled *Stork Book.* I do not think the breed exists today. They chronicled the infancy of my brother and myself. Painstaking entries in my mother's handwriting of weight, diet, bowel movements, first steps, words, teeth, samples from first haircuts were accompanied by photographs of stages of babyhood. I found these books fascinating and faintly disgusting. Why this clinical record? Did my mother keep these pages up to date while starched nurses took over the care of my brother and me? And was her everyday anxiety relieved by clerical busyness, her overlively conscience somewhat assuaged by keeping a faithful log of developments, removed from the din and dangers of actual battle?

In later years, the library was the setting for many of my father's evenings during the last part of his life when he no longer had the strength for his bachelor entertainments outside. Then Daisy Heinz would be ensconced on the worn black and gray brocade sofa under the engraving of Notre Dame. She would sit very straight, her still-shapely legs crossed in ladylike fashion, her thinning hair crimped and tinted smoky blue. She wore too much rouge and her lipstick overran her dainty mouth like the crayon efforts of a child, but her figure had remained slim and she wore refined sober clothes with a gold cross hanging from a long chain.

She tried to fit casually into the brocaded corner, but she appeared ill at ease with a heartiness that was partly defiant. I was both resentful and relieved at the sight of her. What was this woman doing in my mother's place? I could substitute the image of my mother, in a comfortable woolen at-home robe, her face clean of makeup, but still classicly perfect in middle age, with high cheekbones and modeled hollows. She would look up from her book at my father drowsing in his chair by the window after a busy day at the brewery, or sitting at the desk digging out a piece of information from his beloved encyclopaedia, and she would exclaim, "Doesn't your father have the most beautiful mouth!" or, in the same admiring tone, "I think he looks like a Bonzo dog." Whatever species that was, I thought this description more apt, as his brown face had grown pudgy and jowly with the years. But both remarks were delivered by my mother with equal adoration, and although "beautiful" was not an adjective I would ever have applied to any part of that well-known homely face, in some indefinable way I understood my mother and we were in essential agreement. So I would ask myself, what could Daisy be doing here? The answer was promptly returned: she is relieving you of much of the responsibility for your father's old age.

"Hello, Polly," she would greet me, "I haven't seen you in a coon's age."

"How are you, Daisy? You're looking well."

"Tell that to the Marines! But I like to hear it just the same."

I started to move off toward the foyer.

"Now don't go away," Daisy said, "your father will be here soon, but maybe you and I have time first for a nice little heart to gizzard."

When my father joined us, I tried not to notice his shuffling step; he seemed to be attempting to ignore Daisy, garrulous and proprietary as always. Yet we both failed to establish our former status across her curly pastel head. He remained an old man in his eighties and I was no longer his child, but had become that awkward changeling, a protective adult daughter.

This alteration had been accomplished slowly, without my awareness, but it was given its finishing touch just before my father's eighty-fifth birthday. Unsuspecting, I had been summoned to the doctor's office.

"These x-ray pictures show a cancerous growth on the lower portion of the right lung," the doctor said, spreading the plates before me as though they or his words could penetrate the numbness of my disbelief. "But because of your father's age," the doctor continued, "and the possibly slow growth of cancer at his time of life, I have thought it best not to tell him but to let you, your husband, and your brother know, to help me keep the truth from your father."

This compact made me feel ill and guilty, as though the fourway conspiracy could reduce my father even more surely than the blurry blots disclosed by the x-ray pictures. But I acquiesced helplessly, not consciously disagreeing with the doctor and assuming at that moment the new and unwelcome role of protectress.

"It is even possible that he may die from some other cause entirely," the doctor went on, as though imparting a piece of good news.

I thanked him for his help and went outside into the inferno of the summer city street, blinking in the relentless glare, sagging inwardly from the weight of my new knowledge.

We celebrated my father's eighty-fifth birthday at our home in the country. Now it pained me to see him a guest instead of head of the family. I noticed that his neck looked too thin for his collar. But we all carried on as usual — my brother most successfully. Nicholas seemed to be able to dismiss the thought of death and he appeared noisy and amiable, bearing a birthday cake with eight candles on one side and five on the other. I presented my offering, a traveling clock for the trip to Europe my father and Daisy were embarking on the following week. But I feared I was playing my part badly and the thought of the trip, which the doctor had said "by no means should be prohibited," filled me with sad premonitions. My father, though, was looking forward to it with his almost habitual gusto.

I was able to follow him on his travels as I remembered the way from my childhood: some station in false twilight under a high iron-girded smoky yellow-glass dome, the sweating porters with luggage strapped to their bent, blue-smocked bodies, and our family, waiting on the platform like a stranded theatrical troupe. Only my father, the director, would be thoroughly enjoying himself. The rest of us:

my mother, tired and harrassed; my brother, laden with timetables and hotel pamphlets that he collected; Mademoiselle, continuing to issue orders in subdued tones; a bored tutor; the stout, panting Tini — all seemed to be pulling in different directions. At last the train came roaring in, shatteringly close to where we were standing. It seemed that it would gobble us up, masticating us in its huge, oiled, revolving pistons, consuming us in the red glow of its engine. Piercing the restless routine of perpetual travel, I would feel the wild throb of excitement I always experienced at the sight and sound, the deep vibrations of the oncoming monster. Then my father led us all into the first-class carriage. Though we found ourselves inside the beast, it had become domesticated and I always felt more at home in the train compartment than in the hotel rooms that were our destination. When we pulled out of the station night into broad daylight, I imagined the effect we were making as streets and countryside parted for us and we hurtled on, swallowing tunnels and bridges on our way. Inside the wagon-lit we arranged ourselves comfortably. Even my mother seemed to have forgotten her nervousness and fatigue in endless games of solitaire. She had placed her hat on the luggage rack and, for some unknown reason, always wrapped her hair in a turban of net veiling. She appeared quite settled in. But when the train stopped at the first rural station, the excitement began again. My father insisted upon getting off for "a breath of fresh air" and to buy the ham sandwiches sold on the platform. We would all lean out of the windows, exhorting him not to miss the train, as he walked imperturbably up and down, gaily waving at us, ignoring the warning of the departure whistle. Sometimes, with a jerk, the train would slowly start without him and he would have to be hoisted up by a foreign-swearing conductor. I had nightmare visions of plunging ahead to some strange destination without him. But he always managed to make it safely, well pleased at the bit of commotion he had generated, while we acclaimed him as a hero. His small green-brown elf eyes would dance, and he would say, "I don't know what you people were so excited about. I had plenty of time." Then he would distribute the long crisp buttered rolls with ham overflowing their edges like tender pink tongues. In the aftermath of danger averted, the sandwiches had a special deliciousness that has never been duplicated.

He and Daisy would spend several weeks on Lake Como, one of his favorite spots. I remembered the cellar-cool marble hall of the Villa d'Este. I could picture Daisy seated on a regal high-backed chair near the bust of Beatrice d'Este. The princess on her marble pedestal seemed to be surveying, with aristocratic disgust, the debasement of her former home. Daisy's lipstick would be smudged as usual and she would be uncertain about the appropriateness of her resort garb. But as she waited for my father to descend for dinner so that they could make their entrance together (at the stylishly late hour of nine) into the dining hall, where the violins were playing waltzes from her youth, Daisy was happy with this Indian-summer honeymoon snatched before the curtain fell. And her cheerfulness was not feigned.

But I had always actively disliked our summer holidays

at the Villa d'Este. I used to wander, bored and out of sorts, from the vaulted rooms to the ornate gardens bordering the stagnant beauty of the lake. I imagined my father liked to stop here because the palace, though smaller, reminded him of his well-loved Metropolitan Museum. Only here everything was brighter, whiter, the product of a seemingly endless summer. My mother and father (he dressed in his immaculate striped flannels and blazer, the costume completed by the polished cane — last word in useless, rococo decoration) would go for long afternoon drives, while my brother and I would play languidly on the lawn, where the air was more lifeless than in the marble halls indoors, under the supervision of Mademoiselle or Tini. But my mother had left strict orders that we were not to swim in the malarial lake, nor, because of typhoid fever, eat the glowing raw fruit pyramided on tables on the terrace. I sometimes thought wistfully of the Adirondack summers, the healthy welcoming lake and the uncontaminated fruit. One summer I met a girl my own age, the daughter of a famous Italian opera singer. She was fat and swarthy, and although she could not sing, she was the duplicate of her renowned father, now dead. I was proud to be her friend. We played hopscotch on the white gravel paths in imitation of the games we both had known in Central Park, and hid exclusively from her small, pretty, blond half-sister and my brother behind the box hedges and the venerable trees of the garden. Although I have not seen Maria since those days, I still feel a bond attaching me to her as though we had shared, in some other world, the captivity and boredom of prison life.

Not long ago I returned to Como. My husband was on a business trip to Milan and I asked a friend to drive me to the lake. The *autostrada* was new to me and as throughways are connected the world over, I had the illusion that I was back in the United States. We stopped for lunch at a tourist restaurant and in spite of prosciutto, melon, and pasta, I did not feel I had traveled far from Howard Johnson's. When we took to the road once more, the sign reading "Maloja Pass — kilometers" was a relic from the past, a familiar musical refrain heard from a great distance. It was an autumn afternoon with gray skies and a gentle rain that did not fall but seemed to spread and seep. At last we were on the winding road skirting Lake Como. Everywhere the vegetation was exploding like sun breaking through the dark day. Flowers and flowering vines had the lushness of fruit, and fruit grew on the laden trees with the delicacy of flowers. All the colors were overlaid by a faint golden mist, giving the landscape the texture of fine old tapestry. The houses clustered by the water seemed more numerous than they used to be. I asked my friend to point out the Villa d'Este when we came to it.

"There it is," she said. I saw a white building, slightly larger than its neighbors, slightly whiter, but almost indistinguishable. Could this be the palace-prison I remembered? "The hotel is closed now. The season is over, but we can drive around it if you like," my friend was saying.

"No, this is near enough." I did not wish the changes (probably more imaginary than real) worked by time to be brought any closer. And besides, this ripe flowering route was so beautiful that I wanted it to go on indefinitely. This, then, was what my father used to see on those drives with my mother and, at the last, with Daisy Heinz. It was hard to believe that we had ever been together, that I had been here too, unseeing, playing hopscotch on the gravel paths of the Villa d'Este and longing for the pine smell and cold clean water of the Adirondacks.

That autumn when my father returned from Europe with Daisy Heinz his illness was with him like an ever-present companion. He rarely spoke of it, but I was always aware of it, an impostor between him and me. I watched, horrified, as this evil presence took over my father's days. He still traveled to Brooklyn every morning with Kevin, and I would telephone him when he returned as though his hours there were as faltering as his uncertain steps. When I visited him in the evening, I noticed that his polished cane, once an ornament, had become a much-needed prop. Kevin and Kathleen, the waitress, attended him and I was reminded of my grandfather, long ago, humiliatingly supported between Epting and Sophie. Life seems to be lived along a flat extended surface but, actually, the generations move in circles, in eternal repetitions and reoccurrences: Epting-Kevin, Sophie-Kathleen, grandfather-father, father-myself. Kevin had grown older too. He had a wide ruddy face and wore shining rimless glasses behind which his blue eyes appeared magnified in unvarying goodness. Now when he looked at my father, he had the expression of a nurse, proud of her baby's accomplishment: "Your father drove out to the Bronx to see a new bottling depot," or "Don't you think he's walking better today?" Kathleen also had changed. When she first came to work for my mother, she had been a slim, red-haired Irish girl. Now she had grown very heavy, her white arms as broad as pillars, as though her new role and added responsibilities required this increased volume.

After dinner, my father would sit, apparently unseeing, in front of the television set, with Kevin hovering in the background and Kathleen bringing him his pills. My husband and I and my brother would spend time with him, and sometimes the doctor would drop over after dinner for a glass of beer, pretending to turn a useless medical visit into a social occasion. We all played the pretending game — my father, too — but no one was able to dispel the evil presence. My brother did best. When he and my father would argue about the cost of a new billboard or the opening of another brewery on the West Coast, the stranger seemed to grow faint and everything almost returned to normal. My father's face would light up, loverlike, at the sight of my brother's ungainly hulking frame, and he seemed to shrink when Nicholas shrugged himself into a sloppy ulster in preparation for leaving.

One evening my father and I were seated in front of the television, he drowsing, his neck fragile and drooping inside his wide collar, I waiting for the time to go. He woke with a start. "What are those damned fools talking about?" he asked, referring to the television screen. It was a half-hearted attempt to return to the humorous impudence of other days.

"I have to leave."

"Thank you for coming, daughter." And then fumbling in his pocket, he produced a coin. "Have you any money to get home?"

I was about to return the unneeded coin, when I saw this gesture for what it was, one more attempt on my father's part to reassume his former role with me, protector, provider, comforter and, I, once again, the dependent child. "Thank you, father," I said and put the coin in my purse. I bent to kiss his sallow cheek, hoping my embrace would feel more filial than maternal, and hurried across the room. I looked back and saw that his head had drooped again. He was asleep. On my way out, I opened the kitchen door to let Kevin and Kathleen know that I was leaving.

My father's illness progressed at its own erratic pace. Several times we were summoned to attend the end. The door to his room would be closed while doctor and nurse worked inside with complicated life-prolonging apparatus. My feelings were always mixed on these occasions; the desire for his survival opposed a secret wish for a peaceful death that would avert the additional suffering that was lying in wait for him. But Nicholas was always optimistic, noisily banning the possibility of death; to him my father's eighty-seven years were not a death warrant but a proof of immortality. Time and again my father would emerge from behind the closed door, temporarily improved, with a modified revival of his old energy. I watched him incredulously as he returned to us, marveling at the stubbornness of the will to live.

On a cold clear afternoon in January, after one of these

resurrections, my father expressed the wish to see the newly completed Tappan Zee Bridge. Kevin drove us slowly along the Hudson River where blocks of ice were floating, tinted by the rays of a salmon-pink heatless winter sun. The long bridge spanned the river delicately. I watched my father's enjoyment of the feat. "Let's go across it, Kevin," he said, leaning forward and rapping on the window with his cane. His enthusiasm was almost youthful, in spite of his old shrunken body, muffled in woolen scarfs and heavy winter overcoat. Like the January sun on the ice blocks on the Hudson, it could illumine but not kindle. The brewery years seemed to have dropped away and he was an engineer again, delighting in the intricacies of suspension and balance, the subduing of nature by man.

It seemed as though this uneasy life might continue indefinitely. We were growing accustomed to its ups and downs within the reduced domain of illness. The course of disease substituted for experience: loss of weight, blood counts, blood pressure, drugs, x-rays, electrocardiograms took over more and more. At some point, a full-time nurse had appeared and Daisy Heinz regarded her with jealousy as a rival. My embattled father gradually submitted to the regime of the enemy. It was pitiful to see him at table, valiantly attempting to eat, as though the untasted squab or sweetbreads set before him were ammunition that he was too weak to man. Kathleen, in squandering disregard, was using the cut crystal goblets and gold-rimmed china that once were preserved for dinner parties. Now, we sat at hollow feasts, presided over by the shadow of my father.

One afternoon in November, Kevin called me: my father had been too ill to remain at the brewery and Kevin had put him to bed. When I arrived, I found him propped up on his pillows in his old-fashioned white cotton nightgown. I noticed the watch with the fob and jackknife, surrounded by pill bottles, had been placed on the table near him. He was divested, just as Wotan (his horse of long ago) had been relieved, for the last time, of saddle and stirrups when he was too old to go on and was being prepared to be put out to graze. My father and I both knew that the final submission had arrived.

"Sit down, daughter," he said in a surprisingly strong voice, "I want to talk to you." Then, for the first time, he admitted the enemy and I was released from the pretending game. His small eyes, embedded now in dark bags of skin, looked directly at me with their former calm and comprehension that had always made many words superfluous. "I just want to let you know that I'm not afraid of dying. I would like to have lived a little longer — long enough to see my grandson grown up. And each day is still worthwhile — but —" It was his own everyday tone and I was the child again shrinking back from the metaphysical jimjams. My father was in command once more, the commonsensical reassuring presence. Without the help of God, he was facing the implacable fact of his own death. But this lack of any religion was in its own way a kind of family ritual. In this hour my father was vindicating the militant atheism of his forebears and demonstrating that their denial of spirit was not an evasion, but stubborn, unimaginative fortitude — the affirmation of life with all its solid, material pleasures and the unflinching acceptance of its cessation. In spite of sorrow and fear, I was comforted.

I never saw my father again. After that we waited in the library, while he was companioned by the doctor and nurses. We waited in the day and at night — both had lost their distinguishing characteristics. I never reentered my father's bedroom. I allowed outsiders to take over. Was it the horror of witnessing death? Or was it, rather, the wish to carry with me, unspoiled, the memory of our last meeting, to keep intact my final picture of him, when in defiance of illness and age, he had been once more the image of himself that I had always cherished? At any rate, his final hours were unknown to me, nor did I ask the doctor whether he had suffered or had been mercifully asleep when the end came. I preferred to think that he had met death with open eyes, his droll, earthy, wise countenance (real or my creation?) unaltered.

After he was gone, I never crossed the threshold of the apartment again. I kept the watch and chain and the junkman took possession of most of the rest: the pictures of the German beer hall, the Infanta, Notre Dame, the furniture, my mother's grand piano, the world of books. At that time I did not wish to see them, although now I am able to remember them like lost relatives and I would be glad for their presence.

A year after my father's death the brewery was sold. Nicholas protested, with the rest of the Kuppermans on his side for once. But they could not prevail against the superior vote of the La Rivière family. Concern for a business was not suitable to the butterfly life-style of young Christian, and his father and uncle were too far away and the brewery too small for their attention. Also, I could picture the heavy, blue, deceitful eyes of Dr. Hermann Walden and his daughter Charlotte lighting up greedily at the prospect of real money in exchange for the diminishing golden river of Kupperman brew. It disappeared. I no longer have any link with the beginnings in the Ludwigsburg Brewery, its linden-shaded beer garden situated on the side of a hill, the castle and the garrison above, the farmlands below, nor with the dirt-paved brewery yard in Brooklyn, the wooden gate, the old homes and the numerous cousins in that small, vanished German-American world. All are flickers in my memory, the remnants of stories told long ago, and when my generation has disappeared, too, no trace will remain.

With my father's death, the world is a wider, less protected place and I am forced to realize that I am being moved along also. The light on the landscape is changing as it did on those summer trips through the Alps in my childhood. The train would start off in a valley, enclosed by mountains. At their bases chalets were clustered with rocks dotting their roofs for protection against storms. But as I stared from behind the shelter of the train window, the day was always fair. Men and women working in the sunny fields rested on their pitchforks to watch the train go by. Identical blond children lined the roadsides, clutching bouquets of poppies, cornflowers, daisies, and edelweiss, and waved endlessly. It seemed to me that I would be in this pleasant valley forever, but with a sigh, the train plunged into a tunnel and when it emerged, the valley was gone and I looked out on a vista of rock, snow, and sky. The train window was a fragile barrier against such vertiginous space and depth. The air had become thinner and it was already afternoon.

CHAPTER VI

I AM A GHOST WHEN MY THOUGHTS RETURN TO ABANdoned thresholds: the entrance to my grandfather's dark living room, the foyer with the player piano, a certain daisy field in the suburbs, the brewery yard, the house on Sixty-second Street, Tini's cell, a gangplank tilted into the mammoth side of a ship, a vine-smothered door in California, my father's bedroom, in his late years cluttered with memorabilia, a doctor's office, the reception hall of a school. All these have been deserted. One place, alone, has resisted the disloyalty of time. It is still inhabited, still piling layers of living upon old foundations.

My husband has often remarked with satisfaction that five generations of his family have made their home at Jacnor Farm. For me the phrase has little meaning, as the twenty years I have spent here have passed as imperceptibly as one long summer's day.

Although time has been suppressed, space has been deepened and these few acres have developed strata of family history that memory, a somewhat inaccurate archeologist, is empowered to excavate. The entrance to Jacnor Farm (named after Jacob and Nora, my husband's grandparents, who built it) is in Westchester, like the first country home I can remember, only one hour from New York City. But the maple-lined driveway cuts through open fields wild with tall grasses in summer and etched in gray in winter. And our large poodle bounding across the meadows, his tail high as a periscope, often flushes a pheasant or follows the scent of a deer whose lovely flanks you glimpse as he vanishes into the woods.

My son's house rises smooth and white from a clearing. It is at once contemporary and romantic — clean, bold, turreted, and steep, yet candidly open to a carpet of grass and spaced trees beneath which one expects to see a unicorn as in the medieval tapestries at the Cloisters. This shining building houses a new family: father, mother, babies; in relation to me, son, daughter-in-law, granddaughters. Their future is mysteriously linked to my past as my life is dimly connected to those who lived before me at Jacnor Farm. The new house evolves from the old, well-utilized land like a blossoming branch from the gnarled weather-beaten apple tree in the orchard.

Halfway up the road that leads from my son's house to ours is a low stone bridge spanning a small brook, hidden but audible after summer rains or when the snow melts suddenly under a surprising winter sun. Willows bend their feathery grace in the direction of the subtle sound of the water, vainly trying to find their reflections in the meager stream. Since my first view of them, the willows have been thinned out by time and occasional severe ice storms. But the remaining ones suggest those gone and are, along with the stone bridge, what they were: the slightly Oriental trademark of Jacnor Farm. Opposite the bridge is the old stable, now a garage, next, the orchard and the vegetable garden. Then the land rises sharply and our house appears.

One late afternoon in November as I walked from my son's house to ours, I saw the sun explode through its windows like fire. The walls looked charred, like a ship consumed in a blaze. The long house appeared as flat as a paper silhouette, and I expected to see it curl and disappear before my eyes. Before this happens, I must remember, I must put it in writing . . .

The geography of Jacnor Farm has actually changed only in small ways since my arrival. But the sights have altered in my mind's eye with the passage of time, and though I am able to remember the past I cannot relive it through my eyes. The big rambling houses (my husband's parents' home and that of "Granny," the matriarch, which now belongs to us) are the same today, yet different. In their comfortable turn-of-the-century, vaguely Swiss chalet forms, I do not find the houses I first saw on the day I became engaged. But the other senses, less sophisticated and more truthful than sight, can impregnate the present with the past: the smell of lilac, privet hedge, rotting apples, burning leaves, the feeling of soft grass underfoot after walking on gravel, the screech of a pheasant — these are the ambassadors of memory. On that day long ago, my husband and I, two very different people then, wandered hand in hand over the grounds and stretched out on the tender April grass near the tennis court between the two houses. It seemed as though our twined fingers had become the very core of our bodies, and I examined his hands, aristocratic and delicate for such a tall athletic boy, and his small-boned wrists sprinkled with dark hair, as though they held all the secrets of his being.

The tennis court is now unused, overgrown with weeds, and his parents' house stands empty, up for sale. My first view of its interior was sun-filled, crowded with chintz and flowers, smelling of country houses the world over. My husband's mother and father reigned over this smiling, orderly kingdom and made me welcome.

Still hand in hand, we walked across to Granny's house, not knowing that before long it would be ours. How exotic it seemed to me at that time, its atmosphere more old-fashioned than its neighbor's. It held many trophies of the old couple's foreign travels. The years spent in Constantinople, where Grandfather had been ambassador, had left behind a Turkish coffee table, old urns, and a sedan chair (now disappeared) that housed a telephone. At the threshold, a Jewish prayer rug is a reminder of Grandfather's piety, worn thin in succeeding generations but still existing faintly in the faded threadbare pattern of the traditional seven-branched candleholder. Grandfather had died many years before I joined the family. Upstairs, in what we called the "ghost room," once his study, there are numerous prints of Abraham Lincoln and George Washington, attesting to Grandfather's patriotism and his allegiance to the Republican Party he served.

I have often studied his photograph. He is a small, thin

man in a straw hat, wing collar, and white shoes, wearing a black band on his sleeve, in mourning for some long-forgotten kinsman. He has a beard (red in his youth, I have been told), a large high-bridged nose, eyes that are both kind and stern. His wife, all in white, larger than he, is standing well below him on the steps where they are posed.

That day the widowed Granny received us on the screened porch. She had grown immensely stout, and her jowls hung in parchmentlike folds. She reminded me of an ancient turtle. Attending her was her maid, Lisa, and Nero, her disreputable cocker spaniel. Lisa had served my husband's grandparents through all the years of their marriage, in all their dwellings on foreign soil. Herself a native of some obscure European country, she was a gypsy type, swarthy, toothless, and domineering, and she left a musty odor in her wake. She was even more bulky than Granny, with monolithic legs that could still be active in attendance on her mistress. The two old women form in my memory a ponderous odalisque and their image lingers somewhere in the house to this very day.

I remember Granny's sharp black eyes and her long pointed chin, which repeated her mother's and her mother's mother's as shown in the portraits that hang in the house now. At the time of our meeting she was an energetic old woman, audacious and undomestic, more interested in safaris to Africa with the most daring of her grandchildren than in running a house. She left all that to the trusted Lisa. The wicker furniture, the Tiffany lamps, and the painted bedroom suites are Granny's legacy to us; they are her neglected children who have managed, somehow, to survive. And they have acquired with the years a certain charm, accrued from family life, varied but continuous, speaking of the passing generations and the stubborn persistence of inanimate objects.

The jutting screened porches of Granny's house are joined by a terra-cotta tile terrace that used to overlook a rose garden ending in a trellised gazebo. The atmosphere was continental turn-of-the-century, and one could imagine long-skirted elegant ladies with parasols moving in sculptural rectitude along the gravel paths around the geometrical flowerbeds. Instead, two old women, fat and somewhat sloppy, looked upon the well-tended property and its far-flung view with dimming eyes that had seen the dirty, teeming streets of Constantinople and the burning sweep of desert under a relentless sun.

After we took over the house, the rose garden, in the care of old Jerry Malherba, once Granny's undergardener, evolved into a vivid tangle of zinnias, marigolds, petunias, and dahlias. My son and his friends would often race through the riotous beds in search of a lost ball or toy automobile. An unchecked growth of wisteria concealed the gazebo. Behind it a giant elm had risen, its wide branches sheltering the whole garden like a huge umbrella. In the evening after dinner, my husband and I sit on the terrace to watch the width of western sky presenting its moving picture of changing color. Blue becomes pink, magenta, molten scarlet, then dusky gray; cloud formations hurry after one another toward the setting sun. The days grow longer, then shorter, and the stars appear sprinkled carelessly against the black backdrop. The fireflies compete fitfully with their brightness and the tree toads and cicadas form a mesh of small noises. And always the elm tree stood guard, housing numerous bird families; sometimes the tree was alive with their twitterings and hoppings.

Friends often joined us on the terrace, new ones taking the places of old, but the familiarity of the setting and our voices lost in space gave a sameness to these gatherings through the years. At one time a young girl played the guitar and sang in a husky voice. We argued about war, politics, books, and people. Our baby was asleep in his crib upstairs; and then he was with us, his newly deep schoolboy's voice joining the others. And still no time seemed to have passed, nothing had changed very much . . .

One evening as we sat at our places, Ralph the gardener appeared, accompanied by Jerry, retired and almost blind. The wild flowerbeds had now given way to a smooth lawn with a fountain that threw a jet of white water from an Italian urn into a circular basin. The flowers were reduced to a bright border of geraniums, alyssum, and phlox. My husband's parents' house had been sold to a new family who were making changes in our shared sewage system, but no one remembered the place where the cesspools were joined.

Then someone thought of Jerry: he went farthest back. Like a blind oracle, he moved over the well-known land and with unfaltering direction led Ralph to the area where the lid was buried. His cane pointed imperiously to the exact spot, and then he slowly retraced his steps, his mission accomplished, dignified and quietly triumphant in his omniscience. I never saw him again.

Summer after summer we would continue our mosaic of small talk on the terrace. "What is that light on the horizon?" someone was sure to ask.

"We have never known. Best not to know." Distance could transform suburban Westchester into the hills of Tuscany.

"The moon is almost full."

"Tomorrow will be hot, I think . . ."

Late one summer we noticed a change in the elm. Its branches, once so protective, were becoming contorted and withered, like supplicant arms in a death agony. We worked to give it extra water and nourishment, but to no avail. We had to stand by and watch it succumb to the advancing blight. At last, in September, some men with axes were called to chop it down. We averted our eyes from the place where it had been and welcomed the distraction of the move back to the city, where the logs we used in the fireplace that winter were all that remained of our sheltering elm.

Although more hours were spent at the back of the house — on the terrace, the porches, and in the flower garden — the front strikes sharper notes in my memory: the accustomed but eagerly awaited sound of the wheels of my husband's car skidding to a halt on the driveway, my son's first bicycle wobbling down the hill, and the shrill warning of its oversized horn.

The vegetable garden extending toward the slope of the orchard belongs particularly to my husband. On his return from the city, it refreshes him like a beneficent spa. And I believe that it is here that he derives his strongest sense of continuity and family life. I enjoy following him along the orderly green rows, observing the vitality of his walk — each step seems like a contained leap. Together we sniff the delicious aroma of reddening tomatoes and point out the maturing gold of the corn tassels and hardy clusters of Brussels sprouts chilled by the first frost.

We were picking raspberries the evening after our small son's first departure for summer camp. The myriad discoveries hidden in the bushy vines and the growing juicy mounds in our baskets somehow comforted our feelings of loneliness and anxiety. I remember that in the distance we heard the familiar explosion of Fourth of July rockets and we both recalled with nostalgia the miniature celebrations held at Jacnor Farm when our son and his friends waited for it to be dark enough to begin . . .

As I rounded the corner of the house set ablaze by the setting sun that November afternoon, I saw the terrace and garden prepared for the hiatus of winter. The chaise longues were stacked inside the screened porches and the fountain was silenced and swathed in burlap for protection against the cold. Two black fir trees stood sentinel before the gazebo. Now that the elm was gone, they had been revealed in straight outline pointing up into the fiery sky. Severe and melancholy, they gave the garden a formal Italian aspect, like the cypress guarding the cemeteries. For years the fir trees had been blotted out by the exuberant growth of the elm behind them. But strangely, I no longer missed the elm whose busy hospitable branches had seemed so indispensable. I prefer the still, somber beauty of the fir trees. Is one always unwittingly faithless to one's own past, I wondered. But the impassive sky gave me no answer. Every cloud had melted into its glowing, golden reach.